Leadership's Got Everything To Do With It!

"Women's Guide to the Sustainable Leader and Organization"

LaKisha C. Brooks, MS
Ms. Alabama US 2013

ISBN-13: 978-1500586898

ISBN-10: 1500586897

Cover Design: StarChild Graphics

Editors: Dr. Beverly Whitest and LaKisha C. Brooks

Table of Contents

Author's Bio

LaKisha C. Brooks is professional leadership development trainer with over 9+ years of coaching, training and management experience. She has conducted and hosted trainings for various organizations and colleges including Georgia State University, Clark Atlanta University and The Professional Women's Group (A Division of Dress for Success). LaKisha is the CEO of Brooks Enterprise and Consultants, a training and development company whose mission is to prepare women of leadership roles in the workplace. She has a Master's of Science in Administrative Leadership and in 2015 will complete a Master's of Education in Training and Development.

Acknowledgements

Throughout my life, I have had influential individuals who have helped shape and mold me as a leader. Some have served as mentors, friends, teachers and business associates. I would like to express my gratitude to those who played an intricate part in this project.

For being especially encouraging for many years, I would like to thank the best friends in the world: Tracey Lindsay, Nancy Klausner, Sabrina Brawner and Katrina Henry.

To my best friend and the love of my life, Aaron Kindle, you have been my rock and have given me the greatest gift in the world, the gift of fearlessness. Thank you!

A final thank you to the three most supportive people in my life, my parents George and Jeanette and sister, Tabitha. You three have been my biggest cheerleaders in the world. You have been there through all my triumphs and heartaches.

Foreword

People buy into the leader before they buy into the vision. —John Maxwell

Leadership is key to the success of any business, organization or group activity. This book written by Ms. LaKisha Brooks, a recognized leadership and development consultant not only describes what leadership is but also gives you the examples and steps to become a great leader.

I have been working as a business consultant and coach for over 25 years helping organizations position themselves for growth. The very first step in assisting them is to access the leadership of the organization. Not so much how they lead, but how the organization follows. Most people feel that they are great leaders without understanding the basics of leadership.

This book does a fantastic job of explaining what leadership truly is, how to develop leadership skills and most importantly, how to get your team to buy into your vision so they will support you as their leader.

After reading this book, you will be able to determine your personality type and how to apply the principles learned to properly develop your skills of leadership.

I highly recommend it to anyone that has taken on the role as a leader in their organization.

Marc E. Parham
Leading Business Coach
CAPBuilder Network Group

Introduction

Some leaders, experts in the field, etc. argue that leadership is innate, while others believe it is a skill which is developed over time. I believe one can develop leadership skills through education and training; I believe there are those who are born with the ability to motivate and lead. In order to stay competitive in the job market, it is beneficial to have necessary leadership skills. Whether one is in a management or entry level position, this skill is necessary for success. Even if your aspirations are not to obtain a new position or become a leader in your workplace, leadership development should be a vital part of your life. Leadership development does not merely entail learning how to manage others, but also includes other factors such as finding your true purpose, goal setting, building a legacy, communication, conflict management and etiquette. This book focuses on leadership in a professional setting for both an employee and an organization. After reading this book, you will have a clear understanding of what it takes to be a sustainable leader, as well as understand what organizations have to do to ensure they are developing leaders and creating a sustainable environment.

Chapter 1

What is Leadership?

Example: James, a new executive at a major company, is hired to not only fill an open position, but is also called to implement change in his department and produce results that lead to productivity and profitability for the company. He has proven himself as a top performer at a competing company and knows he has what it takes to do the same at the new organization. During his first year on the job, James successfully manages his team, and they are able to exceed a number of production goals. Despite the team's accomplishments, he has yet to get the department to buy into his vision. Many employees feel James does not inspire, motivate and lead them. Throughout this chapter, we will examine James' leadership tactics and determine how he managed to meet and exceed the team's sales goals, but could not effectively lead his team.

What is leadership? Before you can be an effective and successful leader, you must first understand leadership and what it entails. Despite many people's attempt to define it, there never seems to be a clear understanding of the term. Before researching and studying the subject, I merely understood leadership as an act of leading and guiding a team or a group of people to accomplish a task or goal. However, there are other meanings. Leadership is transformational, "the reciprocal process of mobilizing by persons with certain motives and values, various economic, political and other resources in a context of competition and conflict, in order to realize goals independently or mutually held by both leaders and followers."[1] "Leadership is an influence relationship among leaders and followers who intend real changes that reflect their mutual purposes."[2] Jim Kouzes and Barry Posner are experts in the leadership field who believe leadership is not a personality, but are skills and abilities. [3] With these examples, it is safe to say the term leadership has a number of meanings, but one thing is certain, no matter who is defining it, leadership involves both a leader and a follower and some type of relationship.

Characteristics of a leader

Leaders have a number of identifiable characteristics. Leaders empower others, know how to delegate, lead by example, are self-motivated, are effective listeners, are good followers and share a vision.

Empower others- An effective leader must be able to motivate, lead and guide others to reach their full potential. A leader has a genuine interest in molding a follower into a leader. Referring back to James from the example, one of his major flaws was his inability to empower his team. He neglected to realize the potential and strengths of the individuals within his department. He merely concentrated on the company's sales quota and was not aware of other talents employees may have possessed. If he had done so, it could have led to discovering his employees' leadership abilities.

Know how to delegate-An effective leader needs to know the strengths and weaknesses of others so they can properly delegate tasks. You should assign tasks based on someone's strengths, not because you have a job that needs to be done. Delegating others DOES NOT involve telling others what to do because you are in charge.

---

[1] Burns, J.M. (1978) *Leadership*, New York, NY. Harper and Row
[2] Rost, J.C. (1991). *Leadership in the 21st Century*. New York: Praeger.
[3] Kouzes, J. M. & Posner, B. Z. (1987) *The Leadership Challenge*. San Francisco, CA. Jossey-Bass Publishers

Lead by example-If you want someone to follow you, you must set an example. Be the leader you would want to follow. This also involves personifying shared values, and teaching others to model the team's values. [4] For example, if you ask your employees to arrive to work on time, but you clock in 30 minutes late every day, you are not setting an example for others and you are making it virtually impossible for others to follow you. James, the executive in the example, constantly set rules in places, but at times, failed to follow them himself. He would leave events early and was not always punctual for work.

Self-motivated- In order to motivate, lead and guide others, an effective leader must be able to motivate herself FIRST!! You should accomplish tasks and set goals without being told or forced. You should strive for excellence and do so with little or no direction from others.

Effective listener-An effective leader understands when to talk **and** when to listen. Effective listening involves active listening. This means engaging in conversation by giving cues that you are listening. Cues can be verbal and non-verbal. In Chapter 4, we will further discuss active listening and its role in leadership.

Good followers-An effective leader knows how to follow when necessary. A good leader knows there will be times when she may need to rely on her followers to take the lead. If this is the case, the leader may then become the follower.

Shares a vision-You must have a mission or vision that you are working to accomplish. This goal can be as simple as meeting daily sales goals or as complex as implementing a new training program. Regardless of the task, you must be able to share your vision amongst

---

[4] Truesdell, C. (2011). *The Leadership Challenge*.[Review of the book The Leadership Challenge, Kouzes, J.M. and Posner B.Z.]National Clearinghouse for Leadership Programs. Retrieved from http://nclp.umd.edu.p1-6

followers and should be able to motivate them to believe in this vision. It can be extremely confusing trying to follow a leader who has no idea where she going. It can feel like the blind leading the blind.

Empowering others

Earlier in the chapter, we learned that leaders should be empowering others to reach their full potential. Additionally, this is one of the main factors that set leaders apart from managers. Empowering others involves inspiring, guiding and coaching. True leaders enjoy seeing others succeed and work diligently to ensure that happens. One way to empower others is to have an open line of communication and provide feedback. This feedback should be constructive criticism that can be used to help your employees achieve their personal or professional goals. Moreover, this should be communicated in a way that the employee understands the feedback is intended to help, not harm them. There is nothing worse than crushing someone's self-esteem because a message was not delivered effectively. Having an open line of communication can help employees feel comfortable with contributing ideas to management and participating in work processes.[5] Another way to empower others is to trust your employees. Allow your employees to prove they can be leaders, take on tasks, problem solve and make critical decisions. Empowering others involves giving others the freedom to be trusted and fail. If your employee fails, it's okay, use it as a teaching moment. Acknowledge that mistakes were made, but also encourage your employee to keep pushing forward. Additionally, offer suggestions for opportunities of growth and allow your employee to determine what she could have or would have done differently. Empowering others is one of the greatest joys of my profession and my role as a leader. Everyone needs encouragement, guidance and sometimes, a nice kick in the butt.

---

[5] Lipscomb, D. (n.d.) The Advantages of Employee Empowerment. Global Post. Demand Media. Retrieved from: http://everydaylife.globalpost.com/advantages-employee-empowerment-4894.html

Advantages to empowering employees

Empowering your employees can have its advantages.

When employees feel empowered, trusted and valued, they tend to be more loyal to their company. Employees want to continue their careers with their employer and grow within the company. Low turnover is also a result of empowering employees, which in turn, means low new hire and training costs. An empowered employee is a happy employee. Those who love their job have a high rate of job satisfaction. When employees enjoy coming to work, the morale of the company naturally improves. Empowered employees feel free to express themselves and display their creativity in the workplace. Allowing creativity can result in new products, services, concepts, ideas, all of which can increase a company's bottom line.

What is involved in leadership?

Leadership is a complex, ongoing process that takes time to master. There are a number of areas involved with leadership and leadership development. Earlier in the chapter, we discussed that leadership involves more than just leading and guiding a team to accomplish a goal. In addition to leading and guiding, leadership involves effective communication, creativity and innovation, human relations and accepting triumphs and failures.

Effective communication-Effective communication is a one way or two way process. Leaders must be able to clearly relay information to followers in order to accomplish a task. Chapter 4 will further discuss communication's role in leadership.

Creativity and innovation-Leaders understand they must continuously create new ideas for their business. Companies should always be on the cusp of their industry's trends and changes. In addition, leaders know the importance of implementing unique marketing tactics for their business in order to differentiate themselves. In the event you do not own a business, you must be creative and innovation in the workplace. A good leader would ask herself, "What can I do to stand out from others?"

Human relations-Leadership involves knowing how to relate to, deal with and handle situations with people. Interpersonal and intrapersonal communications also play a role in human relations. Leaders realize every follower is different and no two persons should be or can be handled the same.

Accepting triumphs and failures-A successful leader knows and understands there will be successes and failures. The important part of leadership is understanding **HOW** to respond to failures and learn from them. A fruitful person will experience a number of failures throughout her life. No one becomes a great, successful leader overnight.

Additionally, Clifton & Anderson believe the "qualities of a leader are a drive to execute, an ability to relate and integrity; moreover, five basic functions of a leader include visioning, establishing stretch goals, teambuilding, measuring progress and celebrating," [6] one of which we will discuss further in the book.

How can leadership development skills be helpful?

1. With the job market being more competitive than ever, it is important to have the intangible skills to set yourself apart. Leadership development skills can allow you to be a more desirable candidate. Leadership skills can aid in climbing the corporate ladder or even starting your own business.

2. Leaders understand they have a responsibility to make a difference in their community. Furthermore, leaders are open and willing to serve as a pillar in their community.

---

[6] Clifton, D.O., Anderson, E.C. (2004) Developing Leadership Strength in College. The Gallup Organization

3. Having effective leadership skills can help in your educational endeavors. With proper leadership skills, you can obtain advanced degrees, maintain exceptional grades and learn new trades and skills.

4. Setting and accomplishing goals can become a much easier task with basic leadership skills.

5. With effective leadership skills, you can influence others. Influencing someone can be either positive or negative. As a leader, you have the ability to impact others' lives.

Who is a leader? Are you a leader?

The answer to these questions varies depending on whom you ask. Leaders come from all industries, all walks of life, and all backgrounds.

Corporate leaders-Example: CEOs, Directors, VPs

Civic/Community leaders-Example: PTA Member, Neighborhood Watch, Local Little League Sports Coach

Celebrity-Example: Actors, Singers, Athletes

Government-Example: President, Governors, Mayors

Religious- Example: Pastors, Priests, Bishops

Anyone can be a leader; YOU are a leader!

What is your personality type? How can it determine your leadership style?

One factor that determines your leadership style is your personality. Today, more and more employers are utilizing personality assessments in their hiring practices. This is not only done to see how you will fit in the organization's dynamic, but to also determine your leadership potential. Many believe there is a correlation between personality, leadership ability and style.

Some believe that those with assertive, Type A personalities are natural leaders. They are usually no-nonsense, take charge personalities that innately lead others. But the idea that Type A personalities are natural born leaders is not necessarily true. Leaders do not have to command a room in order to be effective; believe it or not, some leaders are passive.

I believe everyone should take some sort of personality assessment to determine best work environments, management styles or career options. All my clients take the DiSC assessment created by William Marston. Marston, a psychologist, determined four main personality traits: Dominance, Inducement, Submission, and Compliance.[7] These personality traits can help determine what workplace environment can best suit an individual. Furthermore, the assessment can serve as an indicator of how someone may handle situations in the workplace. Lastly, the DiSC assessment can gauge the leadership style for a potential employee.

Two of my clients noted the accuracy of the DiSC assessment. One mentioned that because of the results, she can now approach her new employment more effectively in order to become a leader in the organization.

There are also other assessments including Myers-Briggs and Strength Finder. There is no right or wrong or best or worst when it comes to selecting the best assessment for you, only preference.

---

[7] DiSC Behavioral Assessment by Dr. William Moulton Marston(n.d.) Retrieved from: http://www.resourcesunlimited.com/William-Moulton-Marston.asp

There are seven major leadership styles:

Coercive: This leader motivates through threats. They have a "do what I say or else" attitude. This can sometimes be necessary and effective when there is an immediate decision to be made or in the event of an organizational crisis. This leader can be feared and intimidating.

Directing: Decisions are typically made by the leader without little input from others, especially from followers. The communication from a directing leader is typically one-way. This leader typically tells others what to do, not necessarily in a threatening manner, but they can micro-manage.

Pacesetting: This leader may be the hardest to please as they set extremely high expectations for themselves as well as those around them. They expect excellence and nothing less; this is because they view themselves as the standard of excellence. Those who work well with less direction, are self-motivated, and highly skilled may find success working under this leader. However, this leadership style can cause followers to have low self-esteem, especially if they are not innately self-motivated and are set the same high standard as their leader.

Delegating: This leader gives tasks to others while also being involved in the process, mainly to provide guidance. This leader will allow followers to make decisions because they feel comfortable and confident the follower will make effective decisions. Additionally, this leader feels secure in trusting their follower because she has proven herself. Ultimately, all final decisions will be up to the follower, who will also decide how the leader will be involved in the decision making process. This leadership style can cause a leader to become complacent, relying too much on their followers.

Democratic: This leader will allow decisions to be made through consensus. The voting process allows everyone to have a "voice" and a "hand" in the decision making process. Although this style is beneficial in some cases; some followers may feel they are not being heard and their vote did not count. Additionally, leaders may feel powerless in the democratic process.

Coaching: This leader aims to motivate, lead and guide their followers. Their mission is to develop their followers into productive members of their team. Additionally, this leader will give tasks to followers, while also seeking ideas from them. This is an effective leadership style as it allows both parties to communicate in a two way manner.

Supporting: This leader is comfortable allowing the follower to handle important day-to-day endeavors. The leader may offer support to the follower, but ultimately, the decisions and control is with the follower.

Before I understood the concept and meaning of leadership, I was a coercive leader. I told my staff, "It's my way or the highway". It was not until I learned I could be more effective using other methods, did I truly become a leader.

Theory X, Y management

When managing and leading others, it is important to decide what method you will use. Moreover, you should understand different personalities and individuals need to be managed differently. Douglas McGregor, in his book, *The Human Side of Enterprise*, notes two theories to management, which identify employees' motivations.[8] These theories are known as: Theory X and Theory Y

Theory X ideas of employees:

Employees dislike work

Employees must be threaten to perform well

---

[8] McGregor, D. (1960) *The Human Side of Enterprise*. New York, NY. McGraw-Hill

10

Employees do not want to be at work

Employees need to be directed

Pros to Theory X

Employees are pushed to their greatest overall potential

Employees are challenged to perform their jobs to the highest degree

Cons to Theory X

May be hard to work with

May be seen as a micromanager

Theory Y ideas of employees:

Employees are able to empower themselves and direct themselves

Employees like to accept responsibility

Employees enjoy their jobs

Employees all have good motives

Pros to Theory Y

Employees feel comfortable talking with individual

Employees will work hard for individual.

Cons to Theory Y

Can sometimes be viewed as a push over

Can be apprehensive to make important decisions

After reading about both Theory X and Theory Y, you can see there are advantageous and disadvantageous to each. Understand the appropriate time to apply each theory when managing a team.

Leaders vs. Managers

There is a growing misconception that those in management positions are always leaders. This is not accurate. There is a vast difference between leadership and management.

Managers are in certain positions to oversee the logistical tasks of an organization. They understand the processes put into place to ensure an organization runs efficiently. This does not however automatically make you a leader. Leaders are those who work with people and understand human relations. Now you may be asking yourself, "don't managers work with people as well?" The answer is yes, they do, but the main agenda of a manager is to take in consideration the "bottom-line" and the procedures of a company. In order to truly be a successful leader, you must know how to not only manage operational tasks, but also lead, guide and inspire others. If you are a true leader, you would never and should never have to proclaim it; others will do that for you. Referring back to the example, James was a great manager who was able to effectively oversee his department's operational goals and even exceeded the company's quantitative goals, but he was not able to lead and inspire his team. This made James more of a manager and less of a leader.

How to exhibit leadership in the workplace

You do not have to be a manager or even aspire to be a manager to be considered a leader in your workplace. There are a number of ways to be a leader in the workplace.

1.   **Take risks-** Do not be afraid to step outside your job description. This shows you are fearless and understand the risks leaders take. Sometimes taking a risk means leaving your current position. I took the risk to leave my job to start my own business. Best decision of my life!

2.   **Effective politicking**-Some individuals do not agree with office politics, but if done effectively, it can be beneficial in becoming a leader in the workplace. **Remember to stay moral and ethical when politicking.**

3.   **Become an asset**-There is a vast difference in being great at your job and being an asset to your company. An asset stands out from coworkers, and the company will be at a loss with their absence. Being good at your job is just not enough; there are a number of people who are good at their job, but not a lot who are an asset to their company. If you leave your company today, will you be missed?

4.   **Take initiatives**- Do not always wait for someone to tell you what to do. Be creative and anticipate what is needed. Be proactive, not reactive.

5.   **Problem solve**-Problems and situations will occur in the workplace; leaders must know how to take care of these matters in an efficient way. They must make critical decisions to solve unforeseen circumstances.

6.   **Set the standard**-Be an example of excellence. This can be as simple as going to work on time, taking effective notes in meetings or dressing appropriately.

7.   **Do not be afraid to stand out-**There may be times when you may not want to fraternize with coworkers or be involved in groupthink. Remember, you are not at work to make friends. You are there to do a job and accomplish your goals.

Mistakes leaders make

Leaders may do a number of things to empower, motive and lead their followers, but they are not perfect and do make mistakes.

Below are some examples of mistakes leaders can make:

Not actively listening to others- Leaders should know when to listen as well as talk. Just because you are silent, does not mean you are listening. Waiting for someone to stop talking so you can make a comment is **NOT** active listening. Additionally, you should constantly be improving and learning. How can you learn when you are always talking and not listening?

Not accepting responsibility-With leadership, comes great responsibility. You **MUST** assume responsibility not just for you, but for your followers/employees.

Not being accountable for your actions-There will be some failures and mistakes made along the way. You have to take ownership of any mistakes, no matter how egregious.

Failing to realize the potential of others-Leaders should be able to realize the potential of others around them and work to maximize that potential. The mission of an effective leader is to recognize the greatness in all their followers.

Not remaining humble- Just because you are a leader, you are not superior or better than anyone. One day your follower may become your leader.

Managing individuals instead of leading them-Leaders should not try to manage people, but lead them. People are not robots that need to be managed. People must be guided and motivated.

Not realizing everyone should be led differently-Just because a management style works well for one person, it does not mean it works for everyone. Employees and followers **WILL** show you how to lead and manage them.

Need for leadership development

Everyone can benefit from leadership development training. Whether you are a college student, parent or CEO of a Fortune 500 company, leadership development can be advantageous for you. When searching for a job today, you want to make sure you stand out and set yourself apart from other candidates with intangible skills-leadership skills. Though there are a number of important intangible skills, leadership is one of the most important. Furthermore, when you have acquired employment, you still may need leadership development training. Developing leadership skills is an ongoing, continuous process and cannot be developed with a single session or training. Some companies implement leadership development programs for employees to ensure they are constantly learning and growing within the organization.

Not only is the need for leadership development training important, but so is how these trainings are developed and who will implement them. Companies can conduct a needs analysis to answer these questions.

Summary:

After reading this chapter, you should know the pros and cons of the seven major leadership styles, as well as different strategies to be a leader in the workplace. Everyone has the ability to be a great leader with proper training and education. Knowing and understanding how to be a great leader, can aid in effectively leading and guiding others and advancing in your personal life and professional career.

Chapter 2

Finding Your Purpose

One of the first steps in becoming an effective and productive leader is knowing your true purpose. I believe everyone has been given an unique talent that they must nurture and grow in order to maximum their greatest potential. Unfortunately, not everyone has discovered their purpose. This is especially important. No one wants to wake up every morning not loving and enjoying what they do. This can have an adverse effect on your mental and physical being. How can you successfully lead others if you are not happy and passionate about what you do?

How to discover your purpose

Until the age of 16, I always knew I would be a top-notch, no-nonsense attorney. However, during my junior year of high school, I uncovered a hidden talent-public speaking. After attending college for speech communication and even hosting a number of local web, radio and television shows in the Atlanta area, I still found myself unfulfilled. I knew there was a greater purpose for my existence; I knew I was supposed to be remembered for more than just hosting local entertainment shows. It wasn't until a few years ago, when I started working in education, teaching and inspiring others, did my purpose finally manifested itself. Once I accepted my purpose, doors started to open and I have not looked back since.

So how you do find your purpose in life? Discovering your purpose is not always as easy as it seems. You may enjoy a number of things, have talents in a number of areas or just have a passion for several endeavors. **That's okay!** Uncovering your purpose is a process, so taking the time to identify everything you are interested in and are passionate about, is necessary. There are a number of questions to ask yourself to find your purpose.

1. **What do you enjoy doing?** This could be any hobby, from sports, arts and crafts, writing or just about anything. Some of my clients find it hard to really think about what they enjoy. This shocked me; I thought everyone could name three things off of the top of their head that they enjoy doing. Believe it or not, some individuals do not view a hobby as a purpose. They simply view it as something to participate in for leisure, but if it is a purpose, you will view it as fun, not as work.

2. **What would you do if money was not a problem?** Most of us go to a job merely because we have to, not because we want to. We have bills and responsibilities and cannot always actually do what we feel we were designed to do. Because of this, we desert the very thing we should be doing, because we feel we NEED to keep our job. I am not suggesting quitting your job to fulfill your purpose, but I am stating that you will never find complete fulfillment chasing after money. There has to be a greater purpose for your life.

3. **What are your motivations?** When considering this question, think of things in your life that inspire you, that push you, that make you better. Everyone's motivations differ; while some are motivated by materialistic and financial accomplishments, others use family to motivate them. There is no right or wrong when it comes to **YOUR** motivations.

4. **What are your strengths?** Just because you love doing something, it does not necessarily translate into your being great at it. However, just because you

are not good at it now, does not mean you cannot work hard to become great. A great leader can recognize both their strengths and weaknesses and can identify what she must do to turn weaknesses into strengths.

5. **What is your ideal lifestyle?**

When you can identify and visualize the life you want, it can help you better determine your purpose and passion in life. Try to be specific when determining your ideal lifestyle. What kind of car do you want to drive? How many hours would you like to work in a day? Where would you like to live? How many vacations would you like to take a year? Ask yourself these types of questions; it may even help to write down your answers. If you are married or in a serious relationship, it may be a good idea to consider your partner when determining your ideal lifestyle.

How is discovering your purpose important in leadership?

Once you finally reach the peak of self-discovery, it is the most freeing feeling you can ever experience. To wake up every morning, knowing what you were put on this earth to do is indescribable. The moment I found my purpose, seemed like the first day of the rest of my life. I wish for everyone to have this experience, and you can!

When you know what you are destined to do and what you are supposed to be doing with your life, it makes it incredibly easy to lead effectively. Knowing your passion gives you confidence that can be contagious and positively affect others. It can also influence someone else to discover and determine their passion and purpose.

Passion and purpose can also be beneficial in the workplace. Just think about it. How many times have you heard co-workers complaining about their job or the company? They do not like what they do and merely come to work because they have to, not because they want to.

This can be draining on others and bring down team morale. On the flip side, imagine a workplace where individuals come to work because they are passionate about what they do and they know they are serving a purpose. The organizational dynamic can drastically change. More companies should have an open line of communication to determine their employees' passions.

Summary:

Identifying your purpose is one of the most exhilarating feelings you can experience. The journey to discover your purpose is not one that will happen overnight. Be patient and let it manifest itself. The signs will be there! Once you have uncovered your true passion, you will start to live your life with a new found purpose.

Chapter 3

Goal Setting

What is goal setting?

Simply put, goal setting is the process of determining something you want, planning how to get it, and working towards the objective. It serves as a map for your life.

Why is goal setting important?

Every great leader knows that setting goals effectively can lead to success. Not setting goals is like going to a foreign country without a map or a translator. You will have no idea where you are going or what you are doing.

Goal setting is important because:

Setting goals can help organize your life.

Setting goals leads to becoming more confident.

Setting goals helps with productivity in your professional and personal life.

SMART Goals

S.M.A.R.T goal setting is a tool that can help you accomplish your goals effectually. Each of the letters in the word SMART represents a word that describes a goal.

A goal should be:

Specific- You should know precisely what you want to accomplish.

Measurable- Your goal should be able to be measured in some way.

Attainable- Based on current circumstances, time and resources, you should consider whether or not your goal is actually attainable.

Realistic- Your goal should focus on results and have a mission or vision.

Time Bound- Can you accomplish your goal in a certain amount of time? There should be deadlines set to accomplish a goal.

Short Term goals vs Long Term Goals

What is the difference between short term and long term goals?

Short Term goals

Any goal that takes up to two years to complete.

Example: Meet quarterly sales goals

Long Term goals

Any goal that takes over two years to complete.

Example: Obtain a PhD.

How to effectively set goals

What is a goal without an effective plan of attack? **Nothing, but a lot of ideas!** It is extremely important to not only set goals, but to do so in a productive manner. Having a great plan will help to accomplish your goals.

Below are some tactics to help accomplish and set goals:

Vision board/Dream board-This is a fun and creative way to help you accomplish your goals. You can create vision boards with your friends, have vision board parties or use it as a teambuilding activity in the office. Later in the chapter, we will discuss vision boards in greater detail.

Start small- The saying goes "Rome wasn't built in a day". So if Rome wasn't built in a day, why do you feel you can accomplish all your goals at once? **You can't.** Just take your time and accomplish one goal at a time.

Be consistent-Bouncing from one goal to the next without completing a task can only cause confusion and ultimately lead to failure. Stay the course and stay focused.

Reward yourself when a goal is accomplished- There is nothing better than treating yourself after accomplishing a task. For example, if your goal was to lose 15 lbs. and you did so, treat yourself to a new pair of jeans or get your hair cut. **Reward yourself; you've earned it!**

Scratch off goals that have been accomplished- This helps to determine what goals you have accomplished and which ones you need to complete.

Once goals are written down, write methods/tactics to effectively accomplish them- Though everyone does not write down goals, it is a great way to track your progress. You can write down goals in a notebook, use a white board, or use the notes section on your smartphone. When you have the goals written down, jot down methods and ways you can accomplish these goals. For example, if your goal is to meet your sales quota by the week's end, think of approaches you can use to accomplish this goal. Approaches can include generating 20 more leads, calling 75 old leads a day or contacting five old clients a day for five days.

Visualize accomplishing the goals-Sometime you have to "see" yourself accomplishing a goal to believe it can happen.

Have a forecast-Set goals for a certain time period and build upon the last goal you accomplished. I always ask my clients to set goals for one month, three months and six months.

Vision board

A vision board is a collage of pictures, words, phrases, drawings or any illustrations that represents your future.

A vision board can:

Help you visualize your goals

Help you determine multiple goals

Help you find creative ways to accomplish your goals

Serve as a constant reminder to always work towards your goals.

What can you use as a vision board?

A vision board can be a poster board, a cardboard backboard, a wall, anything you can like.

Problems with setting and accomplishing goals

Accomplishing your goals is not always easy. If it were, then everyone would be able to do it successfully.

Here are a number of problems you may encounter while trying to accomplish your goals.

Not overcoming obstacles- Obstacles and roadblocks are an inevitable part of life and there is no way to avoid them. You can, however, learn how to overcome them. Create a plan to counteract any projected obstacles. Ask yourself "How will I handle an obstacle should one arise?"

Taking on too many tasks-One problem many goal driven individuals run into is trying to do too many things at once. Remember you cannot give 100 percent to anything if you are taking on too many tasks. Understand saying no is okay; it can be beneficial to your success.

Not setting realistic goals-We previously discussed that if your goals are S.M.A.R.T. accomplishing them becomes more realistic. If you want to become a C-level executive in two years for IBM and you do not have a degree and have no experience in that field, it is honestly unrealistic to aim that high. You may be setting yourself up for disappointment because you are not being realistic. You may ultimately achieve this goal, but two years may be far-fetched. However, with proper training, education and experience it can definitely happen one day.

Not staying focused- You have to keep your eyes on the prize, distractions will happen; life will happen. This can derail you and keep you from achieving success.

Ethics in setting and accomplishing goals

Accomplishing goals can be extremely rewarding, but your values, morals and ethics may be tested at any given time. Sometimes that "little voice inside", known as intuition, will let you know if you are doing the right thing or making the right decision about a situation. There will be times when you are faced with a choice to make; one that is ethical or one that is not.

Here are some important questions to ask yourself.

Will I cheat to get ahead?

Will I lie to get ahead?

Will I compromise my integrity?

Everyone's idea of morals and values differs. What you may deem unethical, someone else may find it to be acceptable. Values, morals and ethics are determined by a number of factors such as your upbringing and family, religion, even society. Not only do ethics and values vary from person to person, but also from country to country.

Every day, we hear of athletes who took banned substances in order to get ahead. They consumed these "drugs" for years, hoping no one would ever find out, but eventually as the saying goes, "what you do in the dark will finally come to light." When your indiscretion come to light, you then have to ask yourself, "was it worth it?" I am sure if you ask former New York Yankee, Alex Rodriguez or former cyclist, Lance Armstrong, they may tell you no.

How to manage time effectively

Part of successfully accomplishing a goal is understanding how to manage your time. How many times have you set goals and said to yourself, "There is just not enough time in the day; I can't get anything accomplished?" The reason you may feel that there is not enough time in the day is because you are not managing your time appropriately. *If some of the most successful people in the world can make time to accomplish goals, then so can you.*

Here are some ways to manage your time more effectively:

1. **Set aside an allotted amount of time to complete one task at a time**- Research has proven the brain functions better when working on one task at a time.

2. **Prioritize your tasks**-There are a number of ways to prioritize your goals. You can complete tasks by order of importance or order of deadline.

3. **Make a schedule**-Keep yourself on track by making a daily schedule. I try to schedule my day as best as possible. Though

things happen and you are not always able to follow a schedule to the "T", if you have a schedule, it is easier to get back on track when distractions occur.

4. **Eliminate distractions**-Avoid distractions as much as possible. For example, if you are working on a presentation for work, do not try to complete the project while watching your favorite television show.

Action plan for setting goals

I tell all of my clients to be as specific as possible when setting goals.

Step 1. Determine the goal. (Is it long term or short term? Is it personal or professional?)
Example: I want to be top salesperson for the next quarter.

Step 2. Why do you want to accomplish this goal? What are your motivations?
Example: Being top salesperson can put me in a better position to become a sales manager. In addition, the top salesperson receives a $1,500 bonus and I am saving for a house.

Step 3. When do you want to accomplish this goal?
Example: The end of the quarter is on September 17.

Step 4. When will you get started?
Example: Today, June 10

Step 5. How will you accomplish this goal, be as specific as possible?
Example: I will make at least 100 calls or spend at least three hours on the phone per day. I will set at least three appointments per day, every day. I will also contact two of my current clients per week and ask them for referrals. I will make a spreadsheet to track who I contact, when I contacted them and the nature of the conversation. I will also notate whether or not I set an appointment or when I should follow up.

Step 6. What obstacles or roadblocks do you see in the future and how will you overcome them?
Example: I will have to help train three new hires which will pull me away from my book of business for four hours a day for three days. For that week, I will take shorter lunches so I can make additional calls and set additional appointments.

Step 7. Have accountability partners. Accountability partners help you stay on track. They push you to accomplish your goals and challenge you when you want to give up. An accountability partner can be a spouse, friend, sibling, colleague, manager or coach. The key to finding the right partner is finding someone who **wants** to apart of the process with you.
Example: My co-worker and I have friendly weekly competitions to push and motivate each other.

Step 8: How will you reward yourself when you complete your goal?
Example: I will take a mini vacation to Florida!

This action plan applies to any area of your life, including personal endeavors. If you are looking to obtain a Bachelor's degree or lose 10 pounds, put together a solid action plan to make that happen!

Organizations and companies goal setting

Goal setting is not only important for the individual leaders, but also for organizations and companies. As with individual goals, companies have to set S.M.A.R.T goals to have success. They should take the same steps as an individual. When setting goals for employees, managers and leaders set quantitative and qualitative goals for them in order to gauge their performance. Moreover, companies may incorporate assessments to determine if employees have accomplished their goals. Leaders and managers at every level also have goals that have been set by their superiors. So the next time you are frustrated by goals your boss has set for you, keep in mind that they too have goals to accomplish.

Aside from employees, companies set S.M.A.R.T goals for their fiscal year. These goals include yearly budgets, sales projections, charitable contributions, salaries, etc. Fiscal goals are extremely important as they can determine whether or not a company should make budget cuts or increases, layoff or hire new staff, fund new projects, or simply whether or not they should stay in business.

Companies should focus on goals for all aspects of their business, including marketing, consumers, company growth, partnership, services, and products. A method to help determine what goals to set is creating a SWOT analysis. A SWOT analysis is a comprehensive breakdown of the Strengths, Weakness, Opportunities and Threats of a business. Strengths and Weakness are internal, while Opportunities and Threats are external. There is no limit to the number of strengths, weaknesses, opportunities or threats a company can have. A SWOT analysis can be as detailed as possible. When creating a SWOT analysis, companies should include all key members in the decision-making process. Below is an example of a SWOT analysis chart:

Strengths	Weaknesses
Example: Reputation- We have been around for 60 years.	**Example: High turnover-**We have to retain staff; we are losing staff at a rapid rate.
Opportunity	Threats
Example: Adding a new product or service-Due to the overwhelming interest in life coaching, we are able to add life coaching to our list of services	**Example: Competitors-**One of our biggest competitors is expanding and is only a mile and a half from our office.

Once the SWOT analysis is complete, a company can then use this information to establish S.M.A.R.T goals for their business. Conducting a SWOT analysis is not a one-time occurrence. Businesses can utilize a SWOT analysis as often as they deem it necessary.

Summary:

Setting S.M.A.R.T. goals is critical for anyone or any business. It takes detailed action plans, focus and proper planning to ensure effective goal setting. Once this takes place, the chances for success increase immensely. Though we all want to accomplish our goals, do not compromise your integrity in order to do so, because there may be dire consequences.

Chapter 4

Communication

What is communication?

Communication is a process in which a message is conveyed. There are a number of methods to transport a message including verbal, written and non-verbal communication. Communication involves a sender, message, channel (how the message is delivered) and a receiver.

Two most common forms of communication

One-way communication

Sender →Message → Channel →Receiver

This is considered **linear communication** because only one party is delivering a message. This is not necessarily because one party is dominating a conversation. This could also occur when watching television, listening to the radio, reading the newspaper, etc.

Two-way communication

Sender →Message →Channel →Receiver

Sender ←Message ←Channel ←Receiver

This communication model is called **interactive**. This involves the sender and receiver both interacting in communication. This can happen amongst humans, any form of art or a machine.

Transactional communication

Transactional communication is not linear, but circular. This communication method illustrates two people constantly responding to each other by initiating messages and sending responses back and forth. [9] Emails, text messages and Instant Messaging are examples of transactional communication.

Why is communication important in leadership?

As a leader, you will frequently send messages as well as receive them. How a message is conveyed can help or damage a relationship. In Chapter 1, we learned that one major quality of a leader is to be able to lead, motivate and guide followers. A catalyst in accomplishing this is proper communication. For example, if a leader of an organization comes into a meeting yelling, screaming and demanding sales reports from her staff, how inclined do you think the staff will be to provide those documents? Not very likely. However, if she speaks in a more positive, encouraging manner and a lower volume, the staff may feel more at ease and perform for the leader. Remember, no one wants to follow a leader who cannot properly communicate with her followers.

Important rule in communication

The sender should never assume how the receiver is interpreting the message. **Example**. Have you ever been the sender in a conversation and the receiver gets upset about a message you delivered. You quickly reply, "I didn't mean it like that." Now there is potential for unnecessary conflict because of a misunderstanding. Misunderstandings are very common in communication. This occurs when one party delivers a message and the other party interprets the message differently than how the sender intended.

---

[9] The Basics of Human Communication (n.d.) Retrieved from: http://humancommkj.weebly.com/transactional-model.html

How to avoid misunderstanding?

1.   **Actively listening**- This can be done by nonverbal cues, such as nods or face expressions.

2.   **Ask questions**- As the receiver, if you do not understand the message, ask questions to ensure you do.

3.   **Confirmation**- The sender should confirm the receiver understands the message. This can be accomplished with questions such as "Do you understand?" The receiver can also confirm she understands the message by restating it. For example, "so you were saying I need to contact the client to get his new contact information?"

4. **Listen more than you talk-** Apply the 80/20 rule. Listen 80 percent of the time and speak 20 percent of the time.

***Misunderstandings can happen in all forms of communication. (Verbal, Written and Non-Verbal communication)

Verbal communication

Verbal communication involves sounds, speech or linguistics.

The use of verbal communication in leadership is extremely common. One way leaders convey messages is through speeches. Leaders perform speeches on a regular and have to do so in a variety of settings.

Speeches: Styles and Types

There are four main speech styles.

1.   **Extemporaneous**- There is time to prepare, but not always a lot of time. Notes can be used, but there are also impromptu sections

of the speech. This style is more conversational. This is the most effective type of speech.

2. **Manuscript**-This speech style is read word for word, verbatim. This can lead to a monotonous performance and leaves little room for creativity. This is effective when reading documents such as student records, legal documents, medical files or anything where 100% accuracy is a must.

3. **Impromptu**-No rehearsal, off the cuff, spontaneous. You must be quick on your feet. This can be unsuccessful if the speaker is not experienced or comfortable with speaking with no notice. This can also be really interesting and creative if performed properly.

4. **Memorized**-This style is completely memorized, no notes and is rehearsed. This can be ineffective if a speaker cannot recover if distracted or interrupted.

There are four main types of speeches

1. **Persuasive**- A persuasive speech is intended to sell the audience, convince them of something or to get them to do something. This type of speech can also sway someone's decision about a specific issue or topic. Examples of this type of speech are a sales presentation or a political campaign message.

2. **Informative**- An informative speech educates an audience on a specific topic. It is also fact-based and explains or describes something. An example of an informative speech is recapping last week's sales success.

3. **Entertaining-** The primary purpose of this type of speech is to entertain an audience. Though all types of speeches may contain humor, an entertaining speech may include a higher amount. In some instances, the entire speech may be

humorous. An example of this type of speech is a company roast.

4.   **Demonstrative-** This type of speech provides instructions to the audience. This is done in a step by step format to help guide the audience through a process, procedure, function or task. An example of this type of speech is corporate trainings.

Factors that impact how a message is delivered and conveyed

A wise man once told me, "It's not what you say, but how you say it." Though what you say is important, it is just as imperative to understand how you are communicating a message. Here are some factors which influence how a message is delivered **(Paralinguistic)**:

Tone-This deals with the sound of your voice; the fullness and roundness of the voice

Inflection-This deals with articulation and stressing of words.

Volume-This is how loud or soft you speak.

Rate of speech-This is how fast or slow you speak.

Other factors in speech include: beat, rhythm, pronunciation, accent and emphasis

Verbal communication in business

Verbal communication in business is extremely important. As a leader, you are constantly verbally communicating with others; whether it is with employees, colleagues, clients, etc. In leadership roles, you will have to communicate with **anyone** from any background: age, socioeconomic status, educational background, gender, etc. How you convey a message can greatly impact the outcome of any situation.

Written communication

Although leaders must have the ability to effectively communicate verbally, written communication is equally as important. Written communication involves sending emails, text messages, letters and the internet. Written communication is an intricate part of leadership. In a world of social media and 140 characters, leaders must have excellent written communication skills.

Sending emails

Emailing is a quick and effective method to communicate in an instant. Businesses use emails to communicate with clients, employees, vendors, partners, and many others. It can save time and increase productivity. Instead of making repeat calls, you can simply send an email to a recipient. Though emailing is widely used and extremely effective, you must understand email protocol and etiquette.

1. **Avoid all caps**- I cannot count the numbers of times I received a professional email with inappropriate cap usage. All caps indicate you are yelling and are upset. Do not put yourself in a compromising position, NEVER email in all caps for business.

2. **Include a relevant subject-**When sending an email, please make sure you include a subject, and that subject should relate to the body of the email. It should be a short sentence or phrase that explains the nature of the email.

3. **Please edit-** Grammatical mistakes and spelling errors are a no-no!

4. **Know when to "Reply All"-**There is nothing more irritating than receiving emails from everyone in your office because they all hit reply all to a group email sent from a manager. I can

recall times when a former manager sent emails regarding updates on our "book of business" and every person included in the email would send their updates, not to the manager himself, but to EVERYONE. If you are addressing a message specifically to one person, just reply to that person. There is no need to send it to everyone.

Additionally, when you hit replay all, you can send information to others that was **only** intended for one person.

5. **Know when use blind carbon copy (BCC) vs carbon copy (CC)-** When sending an email to multiple individuals, you need to know when it is appropriate to reveal the emails of **ALL** your recipients. Sending carbon copy emails will show every recipient's email address, while blind carbon copy masks the emails. When individuals give you their email addresses for business purposes, they are not doing so with the intentions of having their emails shared with others. Treat emails as you would any other personal information such as phone numbers, addresses or social security numbers.

Social media

Social media is a phenomenon which has immensely changed the face of business. Today, more than ever, organizations can advertise and find new customers on social media sites. Individuals can even use social media to obtain employment and network. In this section, we will learn the pros and cons of communicating on social media.

Pros

Social media allows for instant communication with clients, business partners and others. You are able to have a "relationship" with someone without actually meeting them face to face. Social media can create buzz for your brand or yourself, whether you are releasing a new product or service or announcing an important new hire. Effective use of social media can lead to increased business, revenue and customer rapport.

Cons

Utilizing social media can be extremely advantageous for any leader, but there are also a number of negatives. You must be extremely cautious of how you convey a message on social media; unlike an email where you may reach a limited amount of individuals, social media reaches millions in an instant. In an instant, you can damage your reputation, ruin a business deal or lose your employment.

Non-verbal communication

Non-verbal communication is the most used form of communication. Without speaking a single word, you can convey an immense amount of information via cues and behaviors. There have been a number of researchers and experts who have debated the percentage of non-verbal communication in a message. A leading expert in non-verbal communication, Albert Mehrabian, states verbal communication is seven percent of a message, 38 percent is vocal and 55 percent is nonverbal.[10] Joan Damsey states 50 to 70 percent of communications are non-verbal[11]; while some believe non-verbal communication is 93% of a message. No matter which theory is accurate, non- verbal is the largest form of communication in a message.

There are several types of non-verbal communication.

Eye contact

In the United States, it is considered proper etiquette to look someone in their eyes when communicating. Other forms of eye-contact include:

---

[10] Mehrabian, A. (2007) *Nonverbal Communication.* Aldine Transaction

[11] Goude, J., Derrick, M. (2006) Movers and Shakers. *Advance Healthcare Network for Occupational Therapy Practitioners.* Retrieved on May 10, 2014 from: http://occupational-therapy.advanceweb.com/Article/Movers-and-Shakers-2.aspx

eye rolling, gazing, squinting, looking away (avoiding eye contact) and staring.

Posture

Your posture can convey a strong message. Examples include slouching, folding your arms, crossing your leg or ankles, having your chest out and head up. When I train pageant girls, I always focus on posture; from the way they sit down to the way they stand. Sitting up straight and standing tall can project confidence and assertiveness.

Hand gestures

Some individuals, including myself, use hand gestures and hand movements to emphasize what they are saying. These gestures may include pointing, waving, clasping hands or even a thumbs up. Gestures can be subtle or very obvious. Sometimes if gestures are too obvious, they can be distracting and your audience will spend more time looking at your hands than listening to your message. Regardless of how subtle, hand gestures can accentuate whatever message you are trying to convey.

Appearances

Your appearances can say a lot about you; from the way you dress, to what you wear, to how you wear it. In addition to your dress, other appearances speak volumes including your hairstyle or haircut, choice of jewelry and makeup.

Facial expressions

Facial expressions include winking, raising your eyebrows, pouting or biting lips, frowning, smiling and simply making faces. Facial expressions can help determine your mood or emotions.

Touch

Touching is the most intimate form of non-verbal communication. It can also cause extreme discomfort if you are touched on the arm, leg or shoulder by someone you have just met. I can recall when I first began a career in journalism and my producer constantly told me to stop touching the guests on the back. Though I never thought much of it, she explained to me that everyone is not comfortable with being touched. In addition, touching can be read as "I know you" or "I trust you and I want you to trust me."

Proximity

Most people believe you should be at least one arm's length away from someone when communicating. The amount of space you leave between you and someone else can speak volumes. If you are in a professional environment, do not stand extremely close to someone.

Positive non-verbal cues in the workplace

When in the workplace or in a professional environment, try to use these helpful non-verbal cues.

1. A smile
2. Firm handshake
3. Standing up and sitting up straight
4. Eye contact
5. Slight hand movements and gestures, when appropriate
6. Leaving appropriate space between you and someone else
7. Dressing appropriately
8. Knowing and understanding emotional intelligence
   a. Emotional intelligence (EI) involves monitoring, understanding and reasoning your emotions and well as the emotions of others.

Negative non-verbal cues in the workplace

Avoid these non-verbal cues in the workplace or professional environment.

1. Frowning
2. Rolling your eyes when someone is speaking
3. Looking down when someone is speaking
4. Pointing and wagging your finger
5. Hands on hip
6. Tapping writing utensil
7. Touching someone without permission-(On shoulder, arm, etc., when speaking)

There are a number of positive and negative non-verbal cues you can display in the workplace place and professional setting. These examples only apply to the United States, non-verbal cues in other countries and cultures may mean or "say" something else. Be aware of what you are saying without saying it the next time you communicate with someone.

Summary:

Communication is an intricate part of a relationship, especially between a leader and a follower. Communication can either be linear, interactive or transactional as well as verbal, written, non-verbal. When verbally communicating with someone, try to apply the 80/20 rule, as it can alleviate unwanted miscommunication and conflict. Nonverbal communication is the largest form of communication in any message and can be used to emphasize a message.

Chapter 5

Business Etiquette

Proper dining etiquette for a business lunch or dinner

Business lunches and dinners are a staple in the professional world. This may be an opportunity to close a business deal, obtain a new job, secure new clients, gain an investor or get a new business partner. Though you will be discussing important business matters during these dinners or lunches, your business etiquette and manners will also be evaluated. This is just as important, if not more, than the conversation itself. How you conduct yourself and your manners are crucial in exhibiting professionalism, a key component in being a leader. In this chapter, we will discuss proper dining and office etiquette.

Planning for a luncheon or dinner

1. Reserve your table in advance. Some establishments do not accept reservations. Additionally, others have a rule that all of your party must to present in order to be seated. For this reason, it is important to have **ALL** of your party arrive on time.

2. Prior to selecting a restaurant, be sure to ask for the dress code. Some restaurants have a strict dress code policy.

3. Reconfirm your reservation two days or so in advance, especially if you are expecting more or less guests.

4. Ask your guests if they have any preferences on restaurants or dishes.

5. If possible, try to have a dish selected in advance for your guest(s) since you are recommending the location.

6. Research the restaurant you are choosing.

What to do when you arrive

*A hostess may be called a maître d

1. Provide the hostess or host with the name the reservation is under.

2. Ask if there is a coat check.

3. Ask if any of your party has arrived.

What happens if?

You arrive at the restaurant before your guest? You are to wait for the other party before sitting.

You have leftovers? NEVER, NEVER take home leftovers from a business lunch or dinner.

Note: If you are invited to someone's house and are invited to eat, it is considered bad etiquette not the try a dish.

When ordering

If at a business meeting, do not order dishes such as chicken wings, burritos, etc. Do not order foods where you may have to use your hands. It is bad etiquette and extremely messy.

Please let the waiter or waitress know in advance if you are splitting checks. It can become confusing and overwhelming for the waitress if she has to split the checks at the end of the meal. This may cause a delay in getting the check back to your party. This can be a problem if you are on lunch break and only have an hour.

Close your menu and place it to the side when you are ready to order.

When done eating and ready to pay

If you know you are pressed for time when you arrive at a restaurant, let the waitress know in advance, so they can "drop" the check as early as possible.

When you receive your check and know you are paying with a debit or credit card, have the end of the card sticking out of the card holder, as this indicates you are ready to pay.

Please let the waitress know in advance who is taking care of the check.

Please let the waitress know in advance if you would like to receive change.

Tip at least 15% to your waitress; 20% is great if you can afford it.

Note: Most waitresses make the majority of their money in tips.

Table manners

Below are some instructions to remember for proper table manners. This does not apply to just business lunches and dinners, but in any dining situation.

Do not talk excessively loud- As your mother always says "Use your inside voice". People at the other tables are not interested in hearing your conversations.

Watch your elbows-Elbows are never to be on the table.

Switch fork to right hand after cutting your food, unless you are left-handed-This is the American style.

Do not let your utensils touch the table after you have used them. Utensils should always be on the side of the plate.

Salt and Pepper are "married". Salt and pepper should always be passed together, even if someone asks for only one.

When a woman leaves the table, all men should stand up to excuse her.

Food should be passed from left to right.

Never blow your nose at the table.

What to do if:

If there is a hair in your food or drink, do not make a huge scene. Politely tell the waitress and she will return with a new dish if you like. If you do not want a new dish, that is okay as well. Tell your other guests to continue to eat or drink. The manager will typically offer a gift card or a complimentary meal or both.

If you have dropped your eating utensil, do not pick it up. Tell the waitress and she will do so and return with a new one.

If you have food in your teeth, NEVER pick in your teeth at the table! Excuse yourself and remove the item in the restroom.

These are just a few tips that you can use the next time you find yourself on a business lunch or dinner.

Etiquette when conducting business-Code of Conduct

In the professional and business world, there is a code of conduct to adhere to. There are certain do and don't when conducting business. Below are some important business etiquette tips.

1. **Know the first and last name of the person you are speaking with**- Before you initially address someone by their first name; ask them if it is okay to do so.

2. **Arrive 10 minutes early to any meeting unless otherwise instructed.** −There will be instances where your boss will ask you to arrive at a specific time. This may because they are wrapping up telephone calls or meetings and do know want you to wait or disturb them.

3. **Explain who you are and what you do when presenting a business card**-Just simply handing someone a business card without explaining who you are and what you do is counterproductive. Do not assume someone will just read your business card and instantly want to network or do business with you.

4. **Prepare to take notes during a meeting**-Never attend a meeting without bringing a writing utensil and a note pad. In some cases, you may bring a tablet, but I would not recommend it for every meeting in your workplace. You may want to consult your manager before bringing your tablet.

5. **Speakerphone usage**-Before placing someone on speaker phone, please inform them. Simply state, "I have to put you on speakerphone, is that okay?"

6. **Please do not touch someone else's property**-Even if it is a prank, respect other's property. Sometimes people find it humorous to intentionally misplace a co-worker's car keys or lower someone's office chair. Not only is it not a joke, it is juvenile and does not belong in the workplace. This can quickly turn into workplace conflict.

7. **Limit personal telephone calls and internet usage while working-**As mind-numbing and tedious as work can be, it is not the time or place to handle outside business, to apply to new jobs or simply chat with friends online. This not only applies to those who work for someone else, but especially for entrepreneurs. If you are not self-motivated, you can easily find yourself wasting valuable and productive time doing virtually nothing. There will be times when you have to take personal calls or check personal emails, but be mindful of your time.

8. **Never undermine, criticized or embarrass others in a public forum, especially anyone in an authoritative position.**

9. **Try to return emails within 48 hours, even sooner if it is urgent-**There is nothing worse than waiting on an email reply. It can get frustrating when trying to close a deal or conduct business.

10. **Send thank you notes-**A potential client, partner, employer or associate took the time to speak or meet with you, it is nice to show your appreciation.

11. **Do not enter a closed door without knocking-** A meeting may be occurring or a private conversation may be taking place.

12. **Avoid sensitive topics during business meetings-**This includes religion and politics.

13. **Always turn your cell phone OFF or put it on silent during business meetings-**Ringing cell phones are distracting and unprofessional. If you have to take a call,

excuse yourself from the meeting discreetly and apologize upon your return.

14. **Never walk up and read someone's computer screen from behind-**This is extremely invasive and can make someone feel extremely uncomfortable.

Summary:

In any professional setting, etiquette is extremely important and, in some cases, it is your opportunity to make a first impression. Your first impression is a lasting one. When on a business lunch or dinner, please remember proper table etiquette and manners. What you order, how you eat and how you conduct yourself during a business meal is being judged as much as what you say.

In addition to dining etiquette, there is proper office etiquette you must adhere to. Be mindful of these valuable tips the next time you are at the office. These are the little things that can go a long way.

Chapter 6

Self-empowerment and Personal Wellness

Many leaders utilize much of their time taking care of others or dealing with professional affairs that they neglect what is most important-THEMSELVES! Before you begin to empower others or start another business endeavor, take time to empower and take care of yourself. How can you be an effective leader if you are not taking care of your personal wellness? Others depend on you for guidance, inspiration and results; so the next time you think about neglecting yourself, keep in mind those followers and admirers who rely on you.

Self-empowerment

I define self-empowerment as creating the strength, discipline and freedom to define your best self. This means only you can define who and what you are. You have the power to create and control your own destiny. I am a firm believer that if you want something in life, you have to write a roadmap for success. Almost two years ago, a former boss told me I needed to work three more years in my, at the time, current position to become a trainer for the company. Though I respected his opinion as my superior, I knew I wanted to become a trainer. I had the passion, knowledge, education and skills to be a successful trainer, so instead of allowing his words to define my future, I created my own opportunities. I did not let someone determine my path or journey in life. I wanted to be a trainer, so I took the necessary steps to do so. In addition to creating your own opportunities, you should be strong enough to achieve whatever goals you have set for yourself. Self-empowerment takes immense discipline which has to come from within. **No one can want something for you more than**

you do. Leaders strive to empower themselves and others around them. The ability to empower yourself can be extremely important in the workplace because there will be times where you have to motivate yourself during difficult moments. You cannot expect every manager to motivate you to be your best and to push you to perform your job at a high level; this is your responsibility as well.

How to define your best self

Ever wonder what makes you special, unique and stand out from the crowd? In order to discover this, you much first understand how to define your best self. The one key element to defining this is understanding you can only be who **YOU** are. You cannot be your friend, your mother, your sister, your brother or anyone else. **ONLY YOU!** We all aspire to do other things or look up to others, but you have to be the best at what and who you are now and set goals to be a better you.

For example, if you are working as a cashier at fast food restaurant; do not get upset and complain about it, be the best cashier you can be at the moment and strive to position yourself for a better situation.

Only you can determine your worth and how great you are. If you think you have a terrible job situation and there is no way out, then it is true. If you think negatively, negative things will happen. Remember there is power in your words and your attitude.

How to embrace strengths AND weakness.

Before you can begin to embrace your strengths and weaknesses you must acknowledge that they exist. We are human; we come with the ability to do things that improve our lives, but we also come with flaws. Believe me, no matter how successful we believe we are, we all have things that we could work on. This acknowledgement will lead to helping you figure out your strengths and weaknesses. When understanding your strengths, it is important to keep that strength balanced. An unbalanced strength can become a weakness; anything in excess can be detrimental. Keeping your strengths balanced can be a struggle, because if you are good at something you do it more, right? Understandably; but be able to recognize when it is not being productive and try to pull back.

When dealing with your weaknesses eliminate the word weakness and replace it with "growth area." Weaknesses have such a negative connotation. Think of those areas of your life that we label "weaknesses" as an opportunity to grow and add to your list of strengths. Life is about constantly growing and becoming better people. That growth continues until we take our last breath.

What do you do about the negativities in your life?

When there is a something deemed as a negative, you have to see the bright side of the situation. This is also true for negative things about yourself that you may not like. For example, if you are not happy with your job as a sales representative, instead of gripping and complaining about it, look at the positives the experience can bring. As a sales representative, you may gain great intangible skills, such as; customer service, negotiation, organizational, and communication. These skills may then be used in your next job, your own business, or even in your personal life. If you spend your time focusing on the negatives in an experience, you will only make the experience WORSE! If you think negative, negative things will happen. Similarly, if you think positive, positive things will happen.

Another method to alleviate or even eradicating negatives in your life is to change them. You do not like something about your life, situation or yourself, then CHANGE IT! If you do not make an effort to change what you do not like, then do not complain about it. Albert Einstein once said insanity is doing the same thing over and over again and expecting different results. If you want a different result, you have to change something. What you are doing is not working!!!

How to be confident during adversities

You are dealing with a loss in the family or find yourself homeless with your children or you are losing your house. What do you do? How do you stay confident while facing obstacles in your life? It is easy to get caught up in our problems and forget that there are other things that have to be completed in our lives. There are people that are depending on us to get the job done. So how do we deal with this?

The first thing to do is acknowledge what is going on in your life. Take the time to assess what is going on and figure out how to deal. Remember, no matter how high of a status we have, no matter what position we hold, we are humans and we all have human emotions. Giving yourself a time out is imperative when dealing with adversities. What do you do with kids who are acting out and cannot control their actions? We give them a time out. As adults, we are no different. We must also take those time outs in life as well. During the time out, breathe, thoroughly think about the adversity, and come up with a plan to deal with it what is going on. Time out could mean taking time off from work, taking a mini vacation, exercising, or whatever it is you need to relax.

That brings me to my second point of self-care. Dealing with adversity is hard, but you have to make sure you are taking care of yourself. This does not make the problem go away but it does help you to relax and give you a clearer head to deal with what is going on. Pick up a hobby, spend time with your family, or go for a run. Self-care is about relaxing and taking care of yourself physically, mentally, and emotionally.

The most important factor that helps anyone deal with adversity is having a support system. Your support system is a group of people or person that you turn to when things get hard for you. People that can lift you up, pray for you (if that is what you do), and just be a listening ear. Your support system could be your family, co-workers, friends, church members, work out partners, or anyone active in your life. Whether you privileged to have a support system or not, I also encourage you to seek professional help in your life. An overwhelming myth is that therapy is for "crazy people" or you only go to a therapist when you have problems. The latter could be true, but do we not all face problems at some point in our lives. No matter how big or small you consider your problem, I cannot stress enough how important your mental health is and how important it is to seek professional help.

Seeking a mental health professional is no different from seeing a doctor for a physical or getting a tune up on your car. These things are important and must be done frequently and keeping a check up on your mental and emotional wellness is no different. Others areas of personal wellness include: physical, occupational, environmental, spiritual, social and intellectual. For total wellness, each of these areas should be given proper attention and taken seriously. Understand that this may take time and in some cases, total personal wellness may never happen, but try to stay positive and concentrate on the areas of your life that you are able to control and that are successful.

Taking mental days from work

Sometimes taking care of yourself means taking "mental days" from work. These days are different than sick days. Sick days are typically taken when you are physically sick, but mental days are used when you just need a mental break. I have had to take mental days from work due to stress at home, stress at work and just feeling overwhelmed. It was beginning to negatively affect my performance on the job. I also sought the advice of a mental health professional who suggested I take some days to clear my head and regroup. It was the best advice she could have given me. Not only did I receive support from my therapist (who provided me with a letter to present to my employer), but my employer was also supportive of my decision. The human resources manager also mentioned I could file for short-term disability (STD) if I needed it. My former employer viewed mental health as a form of illness and I could have filed for STD insurance. Fortunately, a long four day weekend sufficed. This is an example of a company supporting and recognizing an employee needing time off for the sake of their mental stability.

Companies' role in employee's personal wellness

In my aforementioned example, I noted the support I received from my employer. It is extremely important that companies recognize and support those who need assistance with their personal wellness. Many companies provide employees with personal wellness services, such as; gym memberships, health screenings, counseling, educational opportunities, any many more. They do this because they understand that in order for their employees to perform at their highest potential, they need to be mentally, emotionally, intellectually and physically healthy. As a leader in an organization, you should know how to identify the signs that your employees may need a confidant, are going through issues on the job or need mental health days from work.

Some signs include:

1. The employee's work performance is unusually not up to par.

2. The employee seems aloof.

3. The employee is confrontational.

4. The employee does not want to participate in team activities.

5. The employee misses multiple days at work.

What to do if you are in a leadership role and you have to take a leave of absence?

If you are a business owner or leader in an organization, how do protect yourself or your business in the event of a medical leave?

Some great leaders note that one of the biggest problems they faced on their journey is relinquishing control. This can be a hard task, as you may feel no one can do the job better than you, no one knows the job better than you, and no one has the same passion as you. This all may be true; but what is also true is unexpected things happen and you are not always prepared. You may have an illness, be expecting a child, or need a mental break. Who will run your business or lead your team if this happens? Will the company suffer? Effective leaders understand they cannot do everything by themselves and must rely on others to accomplish a task. In addition, effective leaders should train their followers to handle the company business as if they were there. Your company, projects or tasks should not come to a halt because you are not available. "The show must go on."

Here are few suggestions to protect you in the event of a leave:

-Appoint certain individuals to shadow you or work as an apprentices or mentees.

-Introduce your mentees to important contacts

-Train your mentees on various jobs

-Relinquish Control!! You cannot do everything yourself, especially if you are not mentally or physical able to do so.

Summary:

Most leaders strive to be the best role model for their followers, but in the midst of doing so they sometimes neglect to take care themselves. Just as it is important to impact the lives of others, you must empower yourself. This includes identifying strengths and weaknesses and learning how to overcome inevitable advertises. Furthermore, you should take the time to focus on your personal wellness, including your mental stability as it can profoundly influence your ability to perform at a high level and impact the lives of others. Businesses also have a responsibility to provide employees with personal wellness programs.

Chapter 7

Globalization and Diversity

Diversity

Diversity includes gender, sexuality, religion, race, age, disability, socioeconomic status, ethnicity and nationality. Understanding and being open to diversity can lead to more opportunities, advancements in your career and if you a business owner, it can greatly affect your bottom line. Although most companies understand the value of diversity in the workplace, not all of them have implemented programs to ensure they have a diverse workforce.

Not only should companies strive for more diversity when hiring for entry-level positions, but also in leadership roles. Minorities are immensely underrepresented in leadership roles, especially women and women of color. Although women land more entry level positions at 53%, they fail to later go to upper management positions; 35% percent go on to director level, 24% to senior vice president level and 19% to C-level.[12] This shows us that companies need to do a better job promoting women. When women are placed in leadership roles, they are extremely effective. Companies that focus on developing and retaining women "tend to have share prices that outperform their competitors".[13] Women should not only be the focus of diversity in

---

[12] Shellenberger, S. (2012) The XX Factor: What's Holding Women Back? *The Wall Street Journal.* Retrieved on June 1, 2014 from: http://online.wsj.com/news/articles/SB100014240527023047466045773819532387 75784

[13] Storrie, M. (2012) The Business Imperative: Recruiting, Developing and Retaining Women in the Workplace. UNC Kenan-Flagler Business School. Retrieved on June 2, 2014 from: http://www.kenan-flagler.unc.edu/executive-development/custom-programs/~/media/3A15E5EC035F420690175C21F9048623.pdf.

leadership roles, but also people of color, international talent and younger talent. Implementing diversity in an organization starts at the macro level and works its way to the micro level where top management and leaders should be involved. It is also important to note that diversity should not just include your company's talent, but also consumers. Companies should implement a plan and programs to foster and promote diversity within their organization. Doing so provides a great opportunity to grow your talent pool and customer base.

How to create diversity in the workplace

1. **Recruiting-**When recruiting for new talent, focus on a diverse talent pool. Consider recruiting on historically black colleges and universities (HBCU) and women colleges. Also consider recruiting online on various diversity website including:
   http://diversityworking.com/
   http://www.hispanic-jobs.com/
   http://www.multiculturaladvantage.com/
   http://imdiversity.com/
   Not only should you recruit in the United States, but also recruit internationally. Some of the best and most diverse talents are international candidates. Lastly, it may also be a great idea to recruit and hire individuals from various professions.

2. **Promote women and minorities to leadership roles-**Promoting women and minorities to leadership roles can encourage other minorities and women to step up and apply for leadership roles, if they are not already. Having a diverse leadership team can possibly lead to a more diverse workforce.

3. **Encourage employees to learn new languages and learn new cultures-**One of the most impactful way to create diversity in the workplace is to challenge employees to educate

themselves on different cultures. Offer employees educational programs or trainings that prepare them for international business or a diverse client base.

Advantages of diversity in the workplace

1. **Increased profits and revenue**-Creating a marketing plan that includes new, diverse clientele can increase your organization's customer base and in turn, increase overall profits. For example, according to Fleishman-Hillard Inc. "women will control two-thirds of the consumer wealth in the U.S. over the next decade and be the beneficiaries of the largest transference of wealth in our country's history"[14]

2. **Reputation-**If a company is known for recruiting, hiring and promoting diverse talent, more diverse candidates will be inclined to work for the organization. Furthermore, clients and the community are more prone to support a company who has a diverse workplace.

3. **Creativity-**Having diversity in the workplace can lead to ideas from a different prospective.

Once a company has implemented diversity in their organization, there are still steps they must take to ensure their plan is effective. According to Elizabeth M. Rice, SPHR, (Senior Professional in Human Resources), companies must learn how to lead and manage a diverse workforce. [15] Training and education must be put in place to create a

---

[14]U.S. Women Control the Purse Strings (2013)Nielsen Newswire Retrieved on April 17, 2014 from: http://www.nielsen.com/us/en/insights/news/2013/u-s--women-control-the-purse-strings.html
[15] Rice, E. (n.d.) The Importance of Recruiting a Diverse Workforce. Innovative Employee Solutions. Retrieved on May 17, 2014 from:

sense of unity among the team despite a diverse climate. Managers and employees should be trained on business etiquette, sensitivity, communications and conflict management across cultures. [16] If there is no time given to properly educate and train a team on diversity, there may be irreparable consequences. This may cause a rift in the team, unnecessary conflict or disorganization. Companies can use their own human resources department to train their staff or they hire outside consultants who serve as Subject Matter Experts (SME).

Globalization

One of my professors in graduate school told me that if a business is not thinking on a global scale, they are not truly maximizing their potential. Though I do not believe every company's business model should include an international clientele, I do understand the importance of globalization. Companies who intend to promote to an international market should understand the culture, economy, buying behaviors, trends, and customers of that particular country. An organization's failure to do due diligence can lead to disaster. Let us use, for example, the merger of the Daimler-Chrysler. Daimler, a German based company and Chrysler, an American based company decided to merger together in 1998. Aside from a lack of teamwork and two egos who got rich off the deal, culture differences was one of the biggest reasons the merger failed. [17] The organizational culture of Americans and Germans differ. Chrysler's atmosphere was more relaxed and easy going, while Daimler was more structured and high stressed. [18] Additionally, there were different views on pay scales and

---

http://www.innovativeemployeesolutions.com/knowledge/articles/diverse-workforce-importance/

[16] Ibid

[17] Krebs, M. (2007) Daimler-Chrysler: Why the Marriage Failed. Edmunds Auto Observer. Retrieved on April 12, 2014 from: http://www.edmunds.com/autoobserver-archive/2007/05/daimler-chrysler-why-the-marriage-failed.html

[18] Weber, R., Camerer, C. (2003) Cultural Conflict and Merger Failure: An Experimental Approach. Management Science. 49 (4) 400-415

travel expenses. [19] The fact that most of the German employees were fluent in English, while most Americans were not familiar with the German language was also an indication that there was a cultural disconnect. The cultural difference was not the primary reason for the failure, but it was a catalyst. Ultimately, the merger ended in 2007; Daimler "end[ed] up actually paying $650 million to unload Chrysler to end its exposure to billions in ongoing losses [and] health care costs."[20]

Another example is EuroDisney. After successfully opening a number of locations across the United States and Tokyo, The Walt Disney Company believed it would be a great idea to open a location in France, more specifically Paris. Though this seemed like a clever idea, The Walt Disney Company failed to truly understand the French culture. For starters, the Walt Disney Company neglected to consider Europeans, especially Frenchmen, regularly consume alcohol with meals when they banned the consumption of alcoholic beverages at EuroDisney. [21] Alcohol is prohibited from all Disney properties. After an uproar, The Walt Disney Company changed its position and allowed alcohol on the EuroDisney premises. Another example of cultural misunderstanding was Walt Disney Company's nativity to the time in which Europeans eat lunch. [22] Unlike Americans who eat lunch at various times of the day, Europeans typically eat around the same time 12:30pm; this caused long lines at lunch and overwhelmed staff.[23]

These examples show the importance of understanding culture when conducting business. Before considering international business or

---

[19] Ibid

[20] Isidore, C. (2007) Daimler pays to dump Chrysler. CNN Money. Retrieved on May 3, 2014 from:
http://money.cnn.com/2007/05/14/news/companies/chrysler_sale/?postversion=2007051408

[21] Yue, W. (2009) The Fretful Euro Disneyland. International Journal of Marketing Studies.1 (2)87-91

[22] Ibid

[23]Ibid

traveling internationally for business, you too must devise a strategic plan.

Here are some important factors to consider when traveling internationally.

Language

Is it an English speaking country? If not, will there be a translator? Should you try to learn or familiarize yourself with the language? I would suggest familiarizing yourself with the language. You do not have to be fluent.

Five dimensions of culture

Psychologist Dr. Hofstede, identified the five dimensions of culture: power distance, individualism, masculinity, uncertainty/avoidance and long-term orientation.[24] Understanding these dimensions when conducting international business or traveling abroad can immensely increase your chances of a successful partnership, merger or simply an international vacation. We will focus on power distance, individualism and masculinity.

In the United States, the power distance between employees and management is relatively low. Employees in the United States seem to view managers as more "equal" than other countries. This would explain why you hear of so many employees "telling off" their bosses or telling their bosses what they will or will not do. This is not the case in other countries were the power distance is much higher. Employees and managers are not seen as equals and there is a greater respect for those in a management position. Let us stop to think for a second. Does the low power distance index in the United States help or hurt a manager's ability to effectively lead? Is there any relation between power distance index and the ability to lead others?

---

[24] Hofstede's Cultural Dimensions (n.d) MindTools.Retrieved from: http://www.mindtools.com/pages/article/newLDR_66.htm

A country can be either individualistic or collectivist and this can make a huge difference in how you approach business in a particular country. Countries such as the United States are individualistic. This means those in the US are typically more concerned with I or me or issues that personally affect them, while collectivist culture focus on groups and the community as a whole[25].

Countries and cultures can also be considered masculine or feminine. This is also important to keep in mind for international business. Masculine cultures and countries tend to be more aggressive, less emphasis is placed on a family and work balance and most important roles in the workplace are held by men. In some cases, women are viewed as inferior, especially in the workplace. Conversely, in a feminine country or culture there is a desire and a push for more women in important leadership roles and there is more gender equality in all aspects of life including the home life.

Summary:

Diversity and globalization are intricate parts of being a sustainable leader and organization. If you are not currently working on being more diverse or introducing yourself to new cultures, languages or ways of life, I suggest doing so. Not only will it benefit your personal life, but your professional life as well. If you are an organization or an aspiring business owner, try developing a plan which includes a diverse workforce or international business.

---

[25] The Hofstede Centre (n.d.) Retrieved from: http://geert-hofstede.com/united-states.html

Chapter 8

Conflict Management

What is Conflict?

Conflict is as a disagreement through which the parties involved perceive a threat to their needs, interests or concerns.[26]

Is conflict always a bad thing?

Conflict is not always a problem; it is inevitable and a part of everyday life.

Conflict management styles

There are five main management styles that can be used when resolving conflict.

Accommodating- One is more concerned with maintaining the relationship and is willing to set her individual goals aside.

Compromising-Parties agree to give up part of her personal agenda to achieve a goal. This is a great solution when the remedy is temporary. This can be a problem if someone jumps to this as a solution before considering collaborating. Both parties may not be completely happy.

Collaborating-This is a win-win situation, which considers both parties. It may take time and patience to come to this conclusion.

---

[26] About Conflict (n.d.) Office of Quality Improvement and Office of Human Resource Development. Retrieved from: http://www.ohrd.wisc.edu/onlinetraining/resolution/aboutwhatisit.htm

Competing- "I win, you lose". " It's my way or the highway". In this strategy, one does not mind losing the relationship in order to win the fight.

Avoidance -Choosing to not deal with the problem, pushing it under the rug. This is a great way to handle conflict if the conflict is seen as a minor situation. This can be a negative solution if the conflict demands attention.

Choosing the right method to handle conflict depends on the level of conflict, the relationship you have with the other party, and how much time you have to remedy the situation.

Types of workplace conflict

As with any area of your life, conflict in the workplace will happen. Below are some examples of workplace conflict.

Employee vs. Employee

Line Management vs. Executive Level (Senior) Management

Employee vs. Line Management

Executive Level (Senior) Management vs Board Members/Stockholders

Employee/Management vs. Customer/Client

Internal conflict

When we traditionally think about conflict, the thing first that comes to mind is conflict with another person, but conflict is also internal. Internal conflict comes from within; it is a struggle and a fight that an individual is having with herself. Internal conflict is not always obvious to others. When I was torn with the decision to resign from my position or continue employment, it was extremely difficult and I even spoke with my therapist about it. I experienced internal conflict, having to consider pros and cons of both decisions. Throughout the course of the decision-making process, no one had any idea of my internal conflict. I did a great job hiding it from my co-workers and management. If you are dealing with internal conflict, whether about quitting your job or feeling inadequate at your position, do not be afraid to consult someone; that someone can be a friend, significant other, co-worker or in my case, a therapist.

Ways to manage workplace conflict

Mediation-Sometimes it nice to get others involved, an unbiased individual; typically someone in Human Resources.

Both parties can agree to speak to someone.

Sometimes an outsider may make the suggestion.

Consider the other person's feelings-Sometimes when we are upset, we only think of our side and what we want versus thinking about the other party. Take a step back and think about the other person.

Actively listen-This is one of the hardest things for people to do in conflict. Most people work so hard to get their point across, they fail to listen to the other person. Those who are not talking and are avoiding conflict by tuning the other person out is also not actively listening. Remember the 80/20 rule.

Avoid certain topics-Do not engage in conversation such as religion or politics.

Use healthy language-Use different language. Example: Instead of complaining try complimenting.

Pick your battle-Ask yourself "Is it worth it?"

Try teambuilding activities-There may be a rift in the company and working together on teambuilding activities may help.

Trainings-Implementing trainings for individuals or the entire organization may be advantageous in resolving workplace conflict.

Speak to HR-Your Human Resources department is there for you. Use them; never be afraid to speak with them about any conflict issues, even if your conflict is with a manager, most companies should have an open door policy.

"Open door policy"-means upper manager and human resources leave their "door" open for employees to have an open line of communication.

Creating a conflict resolution plan

When workplace conflicts arise, and it will, your organization must have a plan to resolve it. If not, the conflict grows and rifts occur, job satisfaction decreases and morale suffers. Sometimes simply talking as a group will not eradicate ongoing conflict. I worked in an environment where the tension and conflict between employees and management was so obvious, it sometimes made it uncomfortable to speak with management. We had numerous team meetings addressing the issues, but because ALL management was not present during the meetings and there were never any changes, the conflict continued. It was not until management ACTUALLY actively worked to change the problem did the situation improve. **It is not just about talk, but action!**

Negatives and positives of workplace conflict

The notion of negative side effects to workplace conflict is widely known, but what most do not know is there are also positive effects.

Negatives

Conflict can lead to destruction in the workplace- Feelings can spread throughout the office and be contagious and toxic.

Too much conflict can lead to high turnover- Employees may quit because they do not want to be in a bad work environment. Employees may also be let go because of conflict.

Conflict can lead to low workplace morale-Employees may dread coming to work, and when they are there they may feel disengaged.

Conflict can cause a loss of productivity- Too much time wasted on conflict can lead to little time getting things done at work.

Conflict can lead to bullying including cyber bullying- A lot of people believe bullying happens to younger people in a school setting, but bullying happens in the workplace as well. This can happen to new employees, employees who do not agree with the masses or employees who are different from others.

Positives

Conflict can lead to healthy workplace competition- There is a chance to push workers in a healthy way as they try to alleviate the problem. For example, the conflict in a company may be raising funds for a program; this conflict can lead to employees participating in a contest to raise money for the company.

Conflict to help resolve unaddressed issues- Some people do not like to talk about conflict unless they have to. When it is brought up, it can lead to a great resolution.

Conflict can lead to creativity-Some individuals are asked to tap into their creativity to create new materials or ideas for a company. This may be a result of a workplace conflict.

Conflict can lead to open communication- At times; conflict can force individuals to converse and start a dialog to resolve it.

Workplace abuse and bullying

We have learned that there are a number of disadvantages to workplace conflict, but one of the most devastating repercussions is workplace abuse. Workplace abuse is a silent epidemic that is growing rapidly. This type of abuse comes in many forms including micromanaging, setting high, unrealistic goals and expectations, threats of termination and intimidation, and discussing an employee's performance with other employees.

Micromanaging

You ever heard the term "helicopter" manager? Well, if you have not, it refers to a manager who is constantly hovering over an employee. He or she may walk by and look at an employee's computer screen and ask what she are doing? They may ask what an employee has been doing the past hour. In some instances, a manager may ask an employee to track their entire day, from how many messages they returned, how many appointments they set, or how many cars they fixed? Micromanaging can contribute to an employee feeling doubted and ultimately, losing confidence in her own ability.

Setting high, unrealistic goals

In every company, employees are required to accomplish goals. There may be a minimum standard an employee must achieve in order to meet expectations. As we discussed in Chapter 3, all goals should be S.M.A.R.T., which includes realistic and attainable. When these goals are set too high and are unrealistic, employees may feel as though they are a hamster on a wheel, constantly striving to achieve goals they can never obtain. For example, if your manager tells you that you have to maintain a commitment rate of 80% for your monthly sales for three months and the company standard is 60%, this can lead to an employee feeling defeated and exhausted, knowing she can never live up to company standards.

Threats of termination and intimidation

There is nothing worse than going to work every day feeling as though it may be your last. Threats of termination can be very subtle or obvious. When a manager does this, they feel the only way to get an employee to perform is to threaten her employment. In a managers' defense, they may not even be aware they are mentally abusing their employees by threating their employment. True leaders, however, understand that intimidation is only counterproductive. Can an employee really give 100% to a company if she is constantly looking over her shoulder wondering if she will be fired?

Discussing an employee's performance with other employees

In most cases, if an employer is dissatisfied with an employee's performance, it is discussed with a management team or human resources. Never, in any instances, should a manager disclose an employee's status with anyone who is not on the management team or human resources. This is especially true if that employee had no idea their performance was being questioned. One of my clients informed me that she was told by a coworker that their manager was speaking about her performance to other employees. Because of this, my client began to question her ability and her job knowledge. She felt violated and lost trust in her superiors.

How to handle workplace abuse and bullying?

As a manager/leader, it is your responsibility to ensure your employees feel safe and comfortable enough to speak with you if they are being abused on the job. You must take the time to address their needs and take their concerns seriously. There must be a willingness to accept that employees may feel abused, especially if the abuse comes from the hands of a manager or leader. Workplace bullying may seem like a new term, but it is in no way a new concept. The archaic method of threating your employees and yelling at them to perform to your expectations can now be seen as workplace bullying.

If you are an employee, have the courage to stand out and speak with your immediate supervisor. Schedule a closed door meeting with your manager and other individuals in a management position and discuss the problem. There will be time where only you and you manager may speak to the issue. I would never advise breaking "chain of command" unless the abuse and bullying was severe, such as sexual harassment or racism. In those extreme cases, the best advice would be to immediately contact your Human Resource department.

If you are being abused or bullied by a fellow employee you can also have a conversation with your immediate supervisor to address the issue. You can remain anonymous or if you would like to resolve the issue with the other party, you can ask for a mediation meeting with management and the other party.

I have experienced some of the things I have written about here as well as witnessed others being bullied or abused. It is never okay. There are ways to handle bullying in the work place. In reality, not everyone is able to terminate their employment because they are dissatisfied with their work environment, manager or the morale of their company.

Forgiving

What is forgiving?

According to Merriam-Webster, forgiving is "to give up resentment of or claim to requital for" or "to cease to feel resentment against."[27]

Though forgiving can help to mend a relationship, there are a number of misconceptions to forgiving.

---

[27] Forgive(n.d.)Merriam-Webster Dictionary. Retrieved from: http://www.merriam-webster.com/dictionary/forgive

Below are some examples of misconceptions of forgiving:

Forgiving is for the other person-Forgiving is always for **YOU**, not the other person

Forgiving is a sign of weakness-It takes a very strong individual to forgive someone who has wronged you. Additionally, asking someone to forgive you can be extremely difficult, but doing so, **is not a sign of weakness, but of strength.**

When you forgive someone, you no longer want to retaliate- It is only normal to want to retaliate, but you do not have to.

Forgiving is easy-One of the hardest things to do is to forgive someone who has wronged you. Forgiving for some is not easy.

Forgiving allows the other person to get away with what they have done-The moment you forgive someone does not mean the other person has "won" or "gotten away" with something. The other person may still be at fault for what has happened.

Forgiving is religious-Some individuals do believe that forgiveness is part of their religious beliefs and it may be so, but the true reason to forgive is unrelated to religion.

Summary:

Conflict will happen in every area of your life, both personally and professionally. The key to conflict is how you handle and respond to it. There are five major conflict management styles that can help resolve any conflict: accommodating, compromising, collaboration, competing and avoidance. In the workplace, if these methods do not work, conflicts can grow and fester and lead to workplace abuse or bullying.

Chapter 9

Entrepreneurship and Sustainability

What is an entrepreneur?

An entrepreneur is a person who organizes and manages a business and assumes the risk of profits or losses of a business.

Steps to starting your own business

There are a number of steps involved with starting a business. I will highlight some of the first basic steps needed to form a business. Without these few actions, you may find it difficult to be completely successful and may be subject to failure. It is important to note, most small businesses fail within two years. Although following these steps will not guarantee success, it may help with ensuring your business is set up properly. Remember, setting up a business is just the FIRST step.

File name and business with the state

Typically this is done through your state's Secretary of State Office.

Try to check your Secretary of State Office website.

Example- Georgia Office of Secretary of State Website: http://www.sos.georgia.gov/

Have a name

This should be a unique name. In the State of Georgia, a name may not be duplicated. In order to avoid duplication, the Georgia Secretary of State Office will ask a potential business to check to see if their name is taken and to reserve a business name. A business name is reserved for 30 days.

Please check with your state.

Obtain an EIN with the IRS

Obtaining an EIN, Employer Identification Number is extremely important for a number of reasons.

1.   To set up a bank account

2.   When hiring new employees

3.   For filing taxes

Setup a bank account

When setting up a bank account and selecting an institution, there are some things to consider.

1.   Are there any bank fees?

2.   What is the minimum balance?

3.   Who will have access to the bank account?

4.   How much is needed to open the account?

Obtain business licenses

Many cities, counties or states require a business license to operate. This is different than receiving a required license in a particular field. For example, cosmetologists, personal trainers and speech pathologists are all required to be licensed in order to be in compliance with their respective field's standards. Business licenses are permits that allow a particular organization and business to conduct business in a particular area, such as; a city or county. Each state has certain requirements needed to obtain a business license.

Please check your particular state for requirements.

Get business insurance.

Most small businesses start with a million dollar small business liability insurance policy. Small business insurance works in a similar way as car or rental insurance; it can help cover the costs in the event there is an accident in which your company is at fault. This is very important when dealing with children. The higher the liability; the more likely a company needs liability insurance. Business insurance is not required, but extremely recommended.

Obtain an attorney

This may not always be necessary. An attorney can assist with business endeavors, contracts, negotiation, lawsuits, filing paperwork, trademarks, patents, protecting intellectual property, etc.

Entrepreneurs can also visit the Small Business Administration for more information on starting a small business.

Different types of businesses

Sole Proprietor

Tax Form to be filed to the IRS (1040 Schedule C)

This is the easiest to complete and is formed by one person. The owner will file business profits and losses her own personal taxes.

Corporation

Tax Form to be filed to the IRS(1120)

"A corporation is an entity which is separate from its owners. The corporation is formed under the laws of the state in which it is operating, with Articles of Incorporation"[28]

Partnership

Tax Form to be filed to the IRS(1065)

"A partnership is a business entity with individuals who share the risk and benefits of business. A partnership may include general partners, who bear the liability for partnership debts and for actions of the partnership. It may also include limited partners who are merely investors and who do not share in the day-to-day operations of the business and who do not share in liability."[29]

S-Corporation

Tax form to be filed to the IRS (1120S)

"A corporation which has the benefits of limited liability of a corporation but which is taxed as a partnership, with the income or losses flowing through to the individual shareholders."[30]

Differences in profit and non profit

Profit companies have a board of directors who are paid.

Non-profits can pay their board, but it is not a requirement.

Non-profits must file for a 501c tax exemption to receive most federal funding and they have to file for this exemption within 27 months of the company's inception.

---

[28] Murray, J. (n.d.) Which Business Type is Best? What is the Difference Between Business Types?. Retrieved on May 1, 2014 from:
http://biztaxlaw.about.com/od/businessorganizationtypes/tp/businesstypes.htm
[29]Ibid
[30] Ibid

Profit companies have shareholders and stakeholders

What is a business plan?

A business plan helps to clearly define the purpose, mission and overall goals of a business. It is typically presented as a formal statement and covers a number of elements of the business.

What to include in the business plan

What is your mission and vision statement?
Who is the target audience?
How will you market?
Who will help you with this business?
What supplies do you need?
How will you get the supplies, if necessary?
Do you need investors and how will you get them?
What is your short term and long term plan?
What are your product/services?
What is your budget?
What are your sale projections?
Will you have employees?
If so, what are their roles?

Triple Bottom Line (Sustainability)

For years, the primary concern of businesses was the "bottom line", making a profit. Although, this still is and will always be a focus of all businesses, there are other factors that make for a sustainable business. These factors include a social and environmental awareness. In order for a business to truly be sustainable, they should be striving to satisfy all the areas of the triple bottom line. The term "triple bottom line" was created by the founder of a British consultancy called SustainAbility. John Elkington believed companies should concentrate on three areas: People (Social), Planet and Profits[31]. If you are thinking about starting your own business or working for a company, keep in mind whether or not your business is sustainable. Although I will not go into great details about the triple bottom line, I will discuss examples of each area.

Examples of People
Giving employees tuition reimbursement for higher education
Providing daycare services for working parents
Providing employer paid benefits

Examples of Planet
Installing energy saving light bulbs in your office
Recycling paper and plastic
Conserving water

Examples of Profit
Increased profit margin
Income taxes
Decreasing overhead costs

"Triple Bottom Line" Scenario

Social "people consciousness" (People)

Company X decides to give employees paid time off for volunteering with nonprofit organizations.

Environmental "planet awareness" (Planet)

Company X donates money to build wells for clean water in third world country.

Economy "financial responsibility" (Profit)

---

[31] Elkington, J. (1997) Cannibals with Forks: Triple Bottom Line of 21st Century Business. Gabriola Island, BC New Society Publishers

Company X is able to make a 4% profit increase for its fiscal year by eliminating unnecessary overhead costs.

Once Company X satisfies all areas of the triple bottom line, they are then considered "Sustainable." Being a sustainable business has a number of advantages.

1. Helps with public image. If a company is known for using recyclable products, most individuals automatically think "They are a great company; they really do care about our environment."

2. Helps with growing revenue. Knowing how to properly manage your funds and eliminate wasteful spending increases the chances of making a profit or growing revenue

3. Sustainability increases employee job satisfaction and retention.

Steps to implement sustainability in the workplace

Conduct a needs analysis

       -Contact a sustainability professional for assistance

Have a planning committee

Set reasonable and attainable goals

Pilot program / (and) Test group

Evaluate results from test group

Though we are discussing sustainability within an organization, you can also be a sustainable person by living a sustainable life. This includes having a consciousness for social, environmental and economic issues in your personal life as well as your community. There are a number of ways to become more sustainable.

Below are just a few suggestions.

1. Avoid using plastic bags when grocery shopping, bring your own bags
2. Car pool
3. Use energy saving appliances
4. Turn off water when you are brushing your teeth
5. Eat less meat
6. Plant a garden

Being a sustainable organization and individual can be extremely rewarding. Remember whatever you decided to do to be sustainable will greatly impact our world and future generations.

Summary:

Starting your own business is not always as easy it seems. There are a number of different steps you need to take to ensure you are setting yourself up for success. Obtaining the right licenses, paperwork and documentation is a great way to aid in this process. When in business, make sure your business is sustainable and you are living a sustainable life.

Chapter 10

Teambuilding

I believe in the saying "teamwork, makes the dream work." But what does that mean exactly? In short, it means in order to see a dream come true, you must effectively work well with others. No matter how successful you think you are or believe you can be, there is no way to achieve all your goals without the help of others. Most successful people have a team of individuals working behind the scenes helping them get to the top. I used to try to do everything myself. Coordinate my own events; write my own bio, market my products, you name it; I tried to do it. I quickly learned that I needed to build a team around me, one I could trust and one who shared my vision.

The same concept applies to the workplace. I know there will be some people that read this chapter and say "I work alone, I don't have to work in groups." This may be true; you may work in a cubicle where you are given an assignment, work independently, complete the project and are on to the next. But no matter how independently you work on projects, your work is just one piece of a bigger pie that impacts the entire team. In order for a business to be success, all parties should be working together to accomplish one common goal. Many performance assessments and leadership competencies measure an employee's ability to work well with others. Working well with others and teamwork involves effectively communicating with others, volunteering for projects, assisting teammates when needed, going the extra mile for the co-workers and the company without being asked.

Why is teamwork important in business?

You are only as good as your weakest link; we have all heard this phrase. If you have a teammate who is struggling to reach her goals how does this affect the overall success of the team? When one person has a deficiency and is not able to keep up with others, it slows down productivity and can greatly influence a business' bottom line. Other team members may feel held back and frustrated. Organizations need to find a way to work with and assist that teammate. One solution is partnering a weaker teammate with a stronger teammate. In addition, leaders within the organization should continue to encourage and support this individual.

How teambuilding activities can be helpful in the workplace

Many companies participate in teambuilding activities to resolve workplace conflict, to help employees get to know one another, to increase morale or sometimes, just to have some fun in the office. These activities can be conducted by the company itself or they may opt to hire an outside consultant.

Teambuilding activities to resolve workplace conflict

When there is conflict in the workplace, teambuilding activities can force staff to interact, work together and possibly engage in conversation. A great way to alleviate or eradicate conflict amongst particular individuals is to place them in teambuilding activities together. Get them to work as a team in a group activity where they will have to trust each other.

Help a team get to know each other better

During organizational changes such as hiring new personnel, teambuilding activities can serve as a great method to introduce new talent. A great example of a teambuilding activity to get to know others in the workplace is Two Truths and a Lie. This is when each person in a group reveals three facts about themselves. Two of the facts are true, while one is a lie. This game can also help reveal similar interests and hobbies which may lead to forming new friendships.

Increase morale

The morale of an organization can be compromised for a number of reasons: conflict, organizational dynamic, staff burn out, job satisfaction, high turnover or job security. When this occurs, typically employees begin to feel stagnant and work begins to feel mind-numbing. This is when a great teambuilding activity can lift up everyone's spirits. I once worked for an organization who arranged a company pot luck in order to increase departmental morale. It was a success! Though it did not eliminate all the problems in the department, it definitely helped to increase morale.

Just for fun!

Teambuilding activities are just plain fun. Negativity does not always have to preface a teambuilding activity. You may just want to engage in an activity because it is fun and you want to do something different.

Teambuilding ideas

1. **Retreats**

2. **Potlucks**

3. **Lock-Ins**

4. **Games**

5. **After work activities, i.e. bowling or dinner**

Pros and cons of working in a group

Working in groups happens very often. In sports, an educational setting, a social setting and even in a professional setting. I must admit, I have not always been a fan of working in groups, but the more I have grown as an individual and a professional, I have learned the importance. There are, however, some pros and cons to working in groups.

Pros

1. Gain interpersonal communication skills

2. Learn to handle conflict

3. Gain knowledge and skills from group members

4. Workload lessened because of team contribution

5. Adapting to others' personalities makes you more diverse to deal with people

Cons

1. Being accountable for everyone in the group

2. Being judged, graded or reprimanded as a group versus as an individual

3. Personality conflicts

4. Limited creativity, your voice may not be heard

5. Groupthink

Groupthink is a "defective decision-making process afflicting highly cohesive and conforming groups"[32] Typically this occurs when a group needs to make a decision, but rather than taking the time to discuss different ideas individually, the group, as a whole, simply makes a consensus decision even if all group members do not agree with it. Members may not want to feel as though they are going against the group. When group think occurs, there is a lack of individuality or creativity amongst a group.

There are ways to overcome groupthink. Some ways are allowing each member to contribute ideas; have their voices heard during the decision making process; bringing in an outside expert or colleague who is not a member of the core decision-making team to eliminate bias. [33]

Summary:

No person or company can achieve success without the assistance of others. Teamwork is an important component to accomplishing goals. Any great leader surrounds herself with dynamic individuals who have an interest in seeing her succeed. Teamwork is equally important in the workplace. However, be conscious of the positives and negatives to working in a group setting.

---

[32] Neck, C., Manz, C. (1994) From Groupthink to Teamthink: Toward the Creation of Constructive Thought Patterns in Self-Managing Work Teams. *Human Relations* 47 (8) 929-952

[33] Lunenburg, F. C. (2010) Group Decision Making: The Potential for Groupthink. *International Journal of Management, Business, and Administration*.13 (1) 1-5

Chapter 11

Networking and Sponsorships

A long time ago, I was told, "it's not what you know, but who you know". Networking is the hidden gem to a successful and promising professional career. This chapter identifies keys to effective networking strategies and how networking, if done properly, can work in your favor.

Keys to effective networking

Some people believe networking is simply going to events and handing out business cards, but there is an art to networking. Networking is a skill that not everyone possesses. But do not fret, if you are not the "queen" of networking just yet, these eight keys will help you master the art of networking.

1. **Remember networking is a reciprocal process**
   "You scratch my back, I'll scratch yours". Networking is as much about giving as it is receiving; it is a give and take relationship. Do not go out looking for individuals to network with only to benefit your own needs and wants.

2. **Have a diverse network**
   Your network should include individuals from various backgrounds including professional industry, age, race and education.

3. **Remember it's about relationship building, not just about collecting business cards-** Collecting cards at an event is NOT a proper method to effective networking. You have to

engage in conversation, build rapport and connect with people. Ask questions. Part of connecting with people and building relationships is being authentic, really listening to the other person. You can ask follow up questions or give nonverbal cues to indicate you are ACTIVELY listening.

4. **Have an elevator pitch-** An "elevator pitch" is a 30 second speech used to tell about yourself. EVERYONE should have an elevator pitch for themselves and their business. Your elevator pitch should not be solely about your title and what you do; it should include your goals, new ideas and talents.

5. **Follow up-** Once you meet someone in person, you must follow up with them. A nice introductory email, if you have their email address, will be a great way to connect with someone you just meet. Not only should you send an email, but you should also find them on LinkedIn, Facebook and other social media. Again, an email to their social media address can prove beneficial.

6. **Host an event-** One of the best ways I network effectively is through hosting events. The events you decide to host can be mixers, parties, trainings, anything! The point of hosting an event is to not only entertain your guests, but to also gain valuable contacts that can be useful to your personal and professional development. Make sure to have a sign in sheet and have attendees RSVP online.

7. **Go to events-**Not only should you try to host events, you should definitely attend them. Make sure to have a plan in place when attending a networking event. Have plenty of business cards, have an elevator pitch, decide, in advance, how many people you want to build some sort of rapport with and make sure these individuals are quality contacts. I typically

assignment my clients the task of meeting 10 new contacts when attending a networking event. Just because you meet someone at an event, does not mean they are a quality contact. Some people believe everyone can be a viable contact, and that may be so, but when you are at a two hour event and there are 100 people and everyone is drinking, talking and mingling, you will not have time to speak to everyone.

You do not need to attend every event in your city. Decide which events will be more beneficial for your overall personal and professional goals.

8. **If at an event, move around!! –**I cannot stress enough the importance of moving around at an event. You are there to introduce yourself, your business or profession, and give someone a reason to want to know you. Try not to spend more than 3-5 minutes with one person before you move on the next person. Leave a lasting impression with the person so she wants to speak more with you later.

Utilizing social media

Social Media is a great way to connect with others. Facebook, Twitter and LinkedIn are just a few websites you can use to network. There are times when you want to use your social media site for personal reasons, and that is okay, but you may want to look into starting a second page specifically for business purposes. These contacts should be those who you can network with professionally. Use these sites to promote your business, accomplishments or activities. Do not forget to add pictures and videos.

Join groups on social media

Joining groups on social media is a great way to connect with other professionals in your field. You can gain invaluable information as well as provide your expertise. Joining a social media group involves more than just hitting the "Join Group" button, it entails participating in discussion and posing questions. When posing a question, make sure the question is open ended and creates interest. It should be a topic that you either are interested in learning more about or a topic you can provided expertise. Other group members may be seeking professional advice or feedback, so it is important to interact with respondents. **Stay involved and active after posting questions!!**

Blogs

In addition to social media sites, you can also use blogs to connect with others. Blogs allow others to get to know you a little better through your writing. Creating an engaging blog can help develop fans and "followers" to add to your network as well as help you become an expert in your field.

How to start a blog?

Determine your blog topic. What are you going to write about? Is it an issue or cause you are passionate about? Will it be a blog about you, your life, your journey, your story? Will you be providing advice or tips?

Select a name. Will your blog have a catchy interesting name? Will it be your name?

Establish a target audience. With any product, you have to have a target audience. Who do you want to read your blog? It is not realistic to think **EVERYONE** will read your blog or be interested. It may also be a good idea to find your niche. Will your audience be women, men, C-level executives, college students, fitness gurus?

Determine your mission statement. What is the purpose of your blog? What message are you trying to convey? What are you trying to tell, sell or reveal? Are you trying to educate your audience or persuade them?

Market your blog. How will you attract your audience? Will you create a social media campaign? Will you start with your current network and work your way out?

Chose a Blog Website. Will you use WordPress, Blogger, Blog.com, Weebly or another site? Familiarize yourself with as many sites as you can and select the best blog website for you. Consider the pros and cons of each site. Will you use a free site or paid one?

What will be your first blog? Your first blog post should catch your audience's attention and draw in followers. It should introduce you, your topic and your mission. Will you have videos, pictures, web links, audio or other multimedia?

Places to network

There are a number of effective places to network.

1. Chamber of Commerce
2. Professional Organizations
3. Work
4. Religious Institutions
5. Educational Institutions
6. Social Organizations

Networking in the workplace

Networking in your workplace is a great way to connect with influential people as well as advance your career. There are a few keys to networking in the workplace. Decide who you would like to network with and why? When I start a new job, I make an effort to schedule a meeting with the highest person in company whose office is in the same building as my office. In my last position, a month after a new president was hired, I scheduled a meeting with his assistant to merely get to know him and introduce myself and my goals within the organization. Not only should you try to get to know the president of your organization, but all upper management. You can gain valuable and insightful information. Trust me, they want to talk you. They want to teach you. All you have to do is ask. One advantage of networking in the workplace is finding a great sponsor.

Why you should have a sponsor? (Don't get a mentor, get a sponsor!)

In the case of professional sponsors, they are individuals who will help guide you through your professional career. They can be someone outside of your organization such as a former professor or a business professional you met while networking. They could also be someone at your current company who is in a management/leadership position. Typically, sponsors have a vested interest in your success especially if they are in your organization. If you succeed, they succeed. They are willing to put their name on the line for you. They are willing to take you under their wing. Sponsors can offer guidance on how to position yourself for advancement, promotions and recognition in your organization. They may ask you to assist on important projects or tasks. One of the biggest differences in sponsors and mentors is sponsors are **actively** trying to help you succeed in your profession. They are more than a role model; they are "fighting" for you to advance in your career. Sponsors will partner with you as you embark on your professional journey. Mentors offer advice, but are more so counselors or a big brother/sister, who serve as role models. They are concerned with your professional growth, but may not actively assist with the process. Important rule of thumb, try to find a sponsor who is at least two management levels higher than you. The best sponsor is someone in a senior or C-level position.

Why become a sponsor?

The real question is why not become a sponsor? All great leaders aspire to touch the lives of others and pay their skills and knowledge forward. What better way to influence the lives of others than through sponsorship. As a sponsor, your job is to prepare mentees to become leaders themselves.

Role of a sponsor

As a sponsor, you role is to:

Prepare your mentee for leadership roles through education, advice, guidance and performance management

Find opportunities where your mentee can display her leadership potential

Suggest your mentee for leadership roles and promotions

How to find a sponsor

Finding the best sponsor is not always as easy as you may think. For starters, the sponsor has to accept the responsibility and want to work as a sponsor. There is no guarantee that because you ask someone to be your sponsor that she will say yes. The first step in finding the best sponsor is identifying individuals who you deem as great leaders. Make a list and answer the question, "What qualities does Joe Doe possess that make him a great sponsor?" Also note any pros and cons of having Joe Doe as a sponsor. Another factor to consider when selecting a sponsor is personality similarities and differences. Just because you think someone is a great sponsor because she was promoted quickly or she has a number of great connections, does not mean she is the right sponsor for you. Determine what personality traits are important to you when selecting a sponsor. Once you meticulously research potential sponsors, identify personality types and your goals, now it is time to solicit a sponsor. Email potential sponsors and describe your interest. Tell them why you are interested and try to schedule a meeting to further discuss the details. Do not get discouraged if you do not hear back or someone declines. It is part of the process. Once you find individuals who are interested, have meetings with them. After the meetings, you have to make a decision and so does the sponsor. If any sponsor says yes, take that as a compliment and accept. Make sure to send thank you notes to everyone, even if they decide they are not interested.

There may even be times when a sponsor seeks you out. She may notice your drive and ambition and decide she wants to see you advance in your career and is willing to help you get there. This is the best case scenario. **If ever approached by a potential sponsor who wants to assist with your professional growth, say yes!!!**

Keys to a successful mentee-sponsor relationship

1. **Keep an open line of communication and have honesty**
   With any relationship, communication is the key. In Chapter 4, we discussed the importance of communication in leadership. In a sponsor-mentee relationship, communication is crucial. You must feel comfortable enough to communicate with one another about important issues. Also, establish an effective method of communication that works best for both parties. Emails, face to face, phone calls, text or video conferences are great ways to communicate. Additionally, each party should provide honest feedback during the relationship. Even if you feel the relationship is

not working out. This will ensure that both parties are learning and growing from the partnership.

2. **Consider each other's time**

    Mentees keep in mind that your sponsor is taking time out of her schedule to help develop and train you. In some cases, you are getting free advice and training from an expert in the field. If you are not able to make a meeting or will be running late, please let your sponsor know. If you have blocked of two hours to meet, utilize that time effectively. Have a plan for each meeting. If you are sponsor, you too, should consider your mentee's time. If you scheduled a meeting with your mentee at 7pm, do not push your mentee to the side if you running over with work or if you do not feel like meeting after a long day.

3. **Set SMART goals for the relationship**

    Before the first meeting, each party should determine their goals for the relationship. During the first meeting, you should discuss these goals to determine how they will be accomplished. Some questions to address are: What is my ultimate goal for this relationship? How often would I like to meet with my sponsor/mentee? What would I like to learn? Are there any challenges I foresee with this relationship? How long will the mentorship last?

Sponsorship programs in the workplace

Some organizations implement sponsoring programs to empower and help develop employees in the workplace. These programs typically involve management, the sponsor and the mentee. Prior to starting the program, the company should determine who will participate, who will serve as sponsors and who will serve as mentees. Will they be selected or will they volunteer? How will the pairs be determined? Personality tests and surveys will be a helpful way to identify which sponsors and mentees may be a great match. It is important to set clear goals and expectations for the program. Some programs may be six months, while others may be yearlong. However long the program, establish how often you will meet. Sponsors should give their mentees homework and assignments on a regular basis. These assignments could include journaling or having the mentee assist on a project. Once the program is complete, management, sponsors and mentees should conduct a follow up meeting to discuss the strengths, weakness and suggestions for the program.

Summary:

Networking is that hidden gem to success. Knowing how to effectively network is a skill that can lead to a number of personal and professional opportunities. A new form of networking is social media. Social media allows individuals to connect and network with virtually anyone in the world. In addition to social media, blogging is also an effective way to acquaint yourself with others. As a blogger, you can serve as an expert in a particular field or just voice your opinion about a certain topic.

Networking in the workplace also has its benefits. You are able to find sponsors or become one. Sponsorships can immensely increase your chances of advancing in your career. Not only do sponsorships benefit the mentee, but also the sponsor. If a mentee excels, so does the sponsor.

Chapter 12

Community Service

Why is community service important?

In Chapter 8, we learned the importance of planet, people and community service for a sustainable business. In this chapter, we will focus on community service for you.

As a leader, it is important to not only be influential in the workplace, but also in your community as a philanthropist and humanitarian. A philanthropist is someone who does good deeds out the "goodness of his or her heart" without seeking anything in return. They have a desire to make a difference in their community by improving the lives of humankind. This can involve environmental, social or political issues. If you think about some of the leaders we all know and recognize, President Obama, Oprah Winfrey or Peyton Manning, all of them do their part to give back to the community, whether it is monetary, donating services and items or by simply making an appearance at an event. No matter the deed, leaders have an obligation to participate in community service. My company, Brooks Enterprise and Consultants, hosts quarterly community service projects. Not only does it help the company with sustainability, but it truly gives me joy to assist others.

Note: When you are a leader, the knowledge and skills you have gained and acquired over the years, should be passed on to future generations. We have to train and mold upcoming leaders. Pay it forward!!!

Ways to give back

There are a number of ways to give back to the community. It does not always involve monetary support, but simple gestures.

Below are a number of ways you can participate in community service.

Help the elderly	Build a garden
Participate in a charity run	Participate in a food drive
Mentor someone	Read to children
Tutor someone	Provide school supplies for kids

What is your cause?

When selecting how and what community service effort to participate in, it may be a great idea to determine what is important to you, why it is important and how you can make a different. For example, you may have a family member with diabetes and you have witnessed them struggle with purchasing expensive medications, now you may want to do something to help raise money for their medication. You may be a person discriminated against because of a disability and now you want to fight for equality.

Every cause does not have to be your cause. You alone cannot save the world alone. Do the best you can to make an impact in your community.

How to plan a community service event?

So you have an idea to host a community service event how do you make it happen?

Many individuals and companies desire to coordinate a community service project or event, but are not sure what to do or even how to do it.

Here are few things to consider when planning a community service project.

1. **What is the name of the event? -** A catchy name can help bring attention to the event.

2. **What is the purpose of the event?** - You have to identify the reason for the event. Are you raising money for something? Promoting or being awareness to a cause? Are you giving out items or providing services?

3. **Who will the event benefit?**-Are you doing this event for someone else as a third party affiliate?; ie The American Diabetes Association, a political candidate, Dress for Success

4. **What is your budget?**-Determine the cost to host the event, as well any profits you may earn.

5. **Who is your target market?** Who do you want to attend the event?

6. **How will you market the event?** How will you reach your audience? Radio, television, social media or hiring a promotional team are useful methods to market your event.

7. **Will you have sponsors or vendors?**-Sponsors and vendors can offset the overhead cost of event.

8. **Will you have partners or do the event alone?**-Partnerships can alleviate the stress of planning and coordinating an event by yourself.

9. **Will you have celebrities or special guest?**-Sometimes having celebrities or special guests can help bring more attention to your event and drive ticket sales.

10. **A run of show-** This serves a schedule and itinerary for the event.

11. **How can you use your network?** —If you have a limited budget, your network can assist with providing resources for the event. Your network can also help with bringing awareness to the event or volunteering.

12. **How much of the money will go back to an organization?**- Some individuals or organizations host events with the intentions of donating a portion of the proceeds to a non-profit organization or a cause. How much of your profits will go back to a charity or cause?

    *Every event does not have to serve the purpose of making or raising money.

13. **Do you need volunteers? -** You can ask friends and family members to assist you by lending their time.

14. **Where will the event be held?**-Decide where you will hold your event. Will it be inside or outside? The number of attendees also determines the event's venue. Make sure to spot check your venue prior to booking it.

Putting on a community service event can be an exhausting, yet rewarding experience. Keep these 14 questions in mind the next time you consider planning and hosting an event.

Summary:

Every leader has a responsibility to give back to her community. This can be as simple as helping someone carry groceries to her car or as grand as hosting a community service event. Whatever you decide to do, just make sure it is done with integrity and good intentions. Doing a good deed should be done because you want to, not because you expect something in return. You will be repaid plentiful for your kind gesture ☺

Chapter 13

Legacy

I view legacy and reputation as the most important aspects of leadership. I have heard many people use the phrase "I only have one life to live, so I am going to live it to the fullest." I agree you should live your life to the fullest; however, make sure that one life is meaningful and has a positive impact on the world. Only **YOU** can determine what path you will take in life and that path can determine the legacy you leave behind. Think about Dr. Martin Luther King, Jr. Think about the legacy he left behind. No, he was not perfect, but he contributed to the world in such an influential way. He produced one of the most famous speeches in American history. He was one of the faces on the Civil Rights Movement in the 1960's. He built a legacy that we will continue to talk about for generations. Another example is Princess Diana. Princess Di, as she was known, was viewed as a humanitarian and community activist. After her fatal car accident, millions across the world mourned her death. Let us take a moment to think about why MILLIONS across the world mourned the death of a woman they had never met. It is because of the legacy she left behind. It is because of the work she did while she was alive.

These are examples of positive legacies. Just as you can have a positive legacy, you can also have a less than stellar one. **Remember, your legacy is totally determined by YOU and only YOU!!!**

Though it is true that you can build your own legacy, it is also true that perception is reality. How does the world view you? At this point of your life, what is your legacy? If I were to ask someone about you, would they respond with a similar answer to what you believe is your legacy? If the answer is yes, then great, you have done an excellent job portraying the image you want to others. If not, then what do you do; how can you change the perception others have of you?

How can you start building your legacy?

Here are some steps to help start building your legacy.

1. Determine how you want the world to remember you.

2. Always remember it is never too early or too late to start writing your legacy.

3. Think about those who will be affected by the legacy you will leave behind. Your children, mother, father, sister, other love ones, friends. You want these people to be proud of you and what you have done.

4. Think about what you have done to significantly contribute to the world- This can be small or large. You do not have to find a cure for cancer to make a significant difference. It can be as simple as donating food to someone or encouraging those in need.

5. Write your own eulogy.

6. If you do not think you have done enough in your life to write the legacy you want; then do something about it.

Reputation

Another aspect of your legacy is your reputation. It always been believed that your reputation precedes you, but what does that mean? This means, whatever society or others think about you is based on YOUR actions or things YOU have done. What is your reputation? Are you known as a giving, hardworking person or are you known as someone who complains and is not a team player? Your professional reputation is just as important as your personal, and at times, they can coincide. Your actions in your personal life can affect your professional reputation, and you should not take your professional reputation lightly. Your reputation can prevent or result in a promotion as well as cause a loss of business or increase new business. It may also lead to termination or workplace conflict. Ultimately, your reputation can harm or help you. **You decide!**

Negative reputation in workplace or business

Example: A talented young executive is extremely hardworking and driven, but her work is out shadowed by her reputation. She is known for being confrontational, aggressive and, at times, crass. Though she continues to excel in her position and her work is impeccable, she constantly finds herself in the middle of conflict with co-workers or management. She has conferences and meetings with upper management and human resources. She vows to not let this become a problem. However, shortly thereafter, she is involved in small spat; though this time she is not at fault and is not the instigator, but because of her reputation, it is immediately believed that she caused the conflict. She attempts to explain her side of the situation, but her manager informs her that because of her reputation and previous run-ins, it is hard to believe she is not to blame for this particular altercation. This is just an example of what can happen if you have a negative reputation in the workplace. You can be a brilliant talent that has a promising future, but because you have such a negative reputation it can get in the way of potential success.

Other ways to harm your reputation in the workplace are:

1. **Being unethical**- stealing time, consistent compliant issues, abusing authority

2. **Quitting your job in an unprofessional manner**- quitting your job without a two weeks' notice (though this is not a requirement, but a courtesy) or quitting your job during office peak season.

3. **Gossiping**-If your name is constantly involved in "water cooler" gossip; people will begin to avoid sharing information with you.

A negative reputation can also cause you to be blacklisted. Blacklisting is an action taken by an employer in an effort to prevent the individual from obtaining future employment[34]. Although this practice is illegal, it does happen frequently to many employees. The biggest problem with being blacklisted is that it is virtually hard to prove and you can find yourself looking for employment for an extended amount of time with no results, not knowing it may be the effect of being blacklisted. Blacklisting is difficult to deal with, and it is never okay to keep someone from being employed, but avoiding a negative reputation can assist with not being blacklisted.

How can social media hurt your reputation?

In an era where technology and the internet are a part of everyday life, more and more people are using these tools to grow businesses, connect with employers or even find their soul mate. Though the internet has immensely changed how we conduct business and interact with each other, we still have to be mindful of what we allow others to know about us via the World Wide Web. Once you put something on the internet, it is there **forever;** and an attempt to "delete" it or "take it down" will not be much help. A simple internet search can retrieve an enormous amount of information about you, so it is essential to be aware of what you are posting. Let us discuss a possible scenario. You are upset with a situation that happened at work between you and your

---

[34] Job-References/Blacklisting (2012) Retrieved from: https://www.shrm.org/LegalIssues/StateandLocalResources/StateandLocalStatut esandRegulations/Documents/Job%20Reference%20Immunity.pdf

manager. Instead of venting privately, you decided to air your "dirt" on the internet, naming the company and your boss. After a number of responses, you think it may not have been the best idea to do this so you quickly delete or "take down" the comment. Because you removed your comment, you think everything is okay. It is not until you are called into your manager's office that you realize the comment has reached her and now your job is at risk.

You have to be conscience of what you put on the internet, especially if you are a leader. Your followers, mentees, employees, subordinators and others are watching you, reading every comment or blog entry. They will watch every video and view every photo you post.

Not only should you be cautious of what you post on social media, but also those who you allow to be active on your profile page, blog or website. Social media sites allow their users to control what is allowed on their pages. You can change your settings to have comments, pictures, videos and other messages approved before anyone else can see them. In addition, it may be a great idea for you to monitor other's activity on your social media page. Watch for vulgar language, profanity, discriminatory or other offensive language. Be mindful and know your social media activity will be scrutinized.

Businesses and reputation

Businesses can also suffer from a bad reputation. How many times have you refused to conduct business at a particular company due to their reputation? My sister recently informed me that she stopped patronizing at a popular fried chicken establishment because they allegedly had not been using "real" chicken. Whether or not this is true, their reputation has already been compromised and it may have possibly affected their bottom line. When a customer or client has a bad experience with a company, they typically tell 10 people about that experience. This is why customer service, great products and services and professionalism is extremely important. With the advent and exponential growth of social media, one bad review or customer complaint can lead not only to a bad reputation, but the end of your business, especially if you are a small business.

Rewriting your legacy

One of the easiest ways to rewrite your legacy and reputation is to hire a top notch public relations firm or publicist. Their primary job is to clean up any "messes" and to ensure their clients have the most positive image. This is a great method for a business or organization, but most of us cannot afford to contract a publicist to clean up our image. There are steps you can take however.

1. Contact those you have wronged or hurt and apologize, mend any broken or burned bridges.

2. Accomplish S.M.A.R.T goals that you have set for yourself.

3. Do a good deed, help someone else!

4. Write down what you want your legacy to be or draw a picture of it.

5. **Be honest with yourself**, have the strength to admit that there are changes you need to make in your life.

Summary:

We all want to leave a lasting impression on the world. Whether it is in our personal lives or professional, the notion of making a difference in our lifetime should be important. The actions we do today, can immensely determine our future. We can, however, take the necessary steps to rewrite our journey if we do not like the path we are on. Businesses too, have to be conscience of their reputation and legacy. If not, this can ultimately lead to a loss in business. Social media plays an intricate part of reputation and legacy in today's world. Be mindful of what you reveal to the world on social media, but also monitor those who have access to your social media accounts. Leave a positive impression on the world!

Conclusion

You have the ability to be a leader in your community and workplace. Leadership and leadership development is essential for you in every aspect of your life, whether personally or professionally. Taking the time to develop and hone these skills can increase your chances of becoming recognized as a leader in your organization.

Although you may be currently in a management role, it does not automatically translate to being a successful and effective leader. Leaders understand that they must not only empower and motivate themselves, but also those around them. Empowering and leading others involves S.M.A.R.T goal setting, communication and teamwork.

In addition to communication, teamwork and goal setting, leaders should also look into and invest their time into finding a sponsor or being one. This is a great way to gain invaluable knowledge from individuals in your field. If you are in a position to sponsor someone, doing so gives you an opportunity to pay your skills and knowledge forward.

One of the most important aspects of leadership is legacy and reputation. In business, your reputation has a way of impacting your bottom line. Keep in mind what you do, how you do it and with whom you do it contributes to your reputation and legacy as a leader.

After reading this book, you are now equipped with the knowledge and tools to better prepare for leadership roles within your organization. If you are already in a leadership position, this guide will help you become a more efficient leader. In addition to personal development, this book serves as a manual to running a profitable and sustainable organization.

Resources

http://diversityworking.com/

http://www.hispanic-jobs.com/

http://www.multiculturaladvantage.com/

http://imdiversity.com/

http://www.sos.georgia.gov/

http://www.irs.gov/Businesses/Small-Businesses-&-Self-
Employed/Apply-for-an-Employer-Identification-Number-(EIN)-
Online

https://www.discprofile.com/

References

About Conflict (n.d.) Office of Quality Improvement and Office of Human Resource Development. Retrieved from: http://www.ohrd.wisc.edu/onlinetraining/resolution/aboutwhatisit.htm

Burns, J.M. (1978) *Leadership*. New York, NY. Harper and Row

Clifton, D.O., Anderson, E.C. (2004) Developing Leadership Strength in College. The Gallup Organization

DiSC Behavioral Assessment by Dr. William Moulton Marston(n.d.) Retrieved from: http://www.resourcesunlimited.com/William-Moulton-Marston.asp

Elkington, J. (1997) *Cannibals with Forks: Triple Bottom Line of 21st Century Business. Gabriola Island*, BC New Society Publishers

Forgive(n.d.)Merriam-Webster Dictionary. Retrieved from: http://www.merriam-webster.com/dictionary/forgive

Goude, J., Derrick, M. (2006) Movers and Shakers. *Advance Healthcare Network for Occupational Therapy Practitioners*. Retrieved on May 10, 2014 from: http://occupational-therapy.advanceweb.com/Article/Movers-and-Shakers-2.aspx

Hofstede's Cultural Dimensions (n.d) MindTools.Retrieved from: http://www.mindtools.com/pages/article/newLDR_66.htm

Isidore, C. (2007) Daimler pays to dump Chrysler. *CNN Money*. Retrieved on May 3, 2014 from: http://money.cnn.com/2007/05/14/news/companies/chrysler_sale/?postversion=2007051408

Job-References/Blacklisting (2012) Retrieved from: https://www.shrm.org/LegalIssues/StateandLocalResources/S

tateandLocalStatutesandRegulations/Documents/Job%20Refer
ence%20Immunity.pdf

Kouzes, J. M. & Posner, B. Z. (1987) *The Leadership Challenge.* San
Francisco, CA. Jossey-Bass

Krebs, M. (2007) Daimler-Chrysler: Why the Marriage Failed.
Edmunds Auto Observer. Retrieved on April 12, 2014 from:
http://www.edmunds.com/autoobserver-
archive/2007/05/daimler-chrysler-why-the-marriage-
failed.html

Lipscomb, D. (n.d.) The Advantages of Employee Empowerment.
Global Post. Demand Media. Retrieved on April 4, 2014 from:
http://everydaylife.globalpost.com/advantages-employee-
empowerment-4894.html

Lunenburg, F. C. (2010) Group Decision Making: The Potential for
Groupthink. *International Journal of Management, Business, and
Administration.*13 (1) 1-5

Mehrabian, A. (2007) *Nonverbal Communication.* Aldine Transaction

McGregor, D. (1960) *The Human Side of Enterprise.* New York, NY.
McGraw-Hill

Murray, J. (n.d.) Which Business Type is Best? What is the Difference
Between Business Types?. Retrieved on May 1, 2014 from:
http://biztaxlaw.about.com/od/businessorganizationtypes/tp/
businesstypes.htm

Neck, C., Manz, C. (1994) From Groupthink to Teamthink: Toward
the Creation of Constructive Thought Patterns in Self-
Managing Work Teams. *Human Relations* 47 (8) 929-952

Rice, E. (n.d.) The Importance of Recruiting a Diverse Workforce.
Innovative Employee Solutions. Retrieved on May 17, 2014

from:
http://www.innovativeemployeesolutions.com/knowledge/arti
cles/diverse-workforce-importance/

Rost, J.C. (1991). *Leadership in the 21st Century.* New York, NY. Praeger.

Shellenberger, S. (2012) The XX Factor: What's Holding Women
Back? *The Wall Street Journal.* Retrieved on June 1, 2014 from:
http://online.wsj.com/news/articles/SB100014240527023047
46604577381953238775784

Storrie, M. (2012) The Business Imperative: Recruiting, Developing
and Retaining Women in the Workplace. UNC Kenan-Flagler
Business School. Retrieved on June 2, 2014 from:
http://www.kenan-flagler.unc.edu/executive-
development/custom-
programs/~/media/3A15E5EC035F420690175C21F9048623.
pdf.

The Basics of Human Communication (n.d.) Retrieved from:
http://humancommkj.weebly.com/transactional-model.html

The Hofstede Centre (n.d.) Retrieved from: http://geert-
hofstede.com/united-states.html

Truesdell, C. (2011). *The Leadership Challenge.*[Review of the book The
Leadership Challenge, Kouzes, J.M. and Posner B.Z.]National
Clearinghouse for Leadership Programs. Retrieved from
http://nclp.umd.edu.p1-6

U.S. Women Control the Purse Strings (2013) Nielsen Newswire.
Retrieved on April 17, 2014 from:
http://www.nielsen.com/us/en/insights/news/2013/u-s--
women-control-the-purse-strings.html

Weber, R., Camerer, C. (2003) Cultural Conflict and Merger Failure: An
Experimental Approach. *Management Science.* 49 (4) 400-415

Yue, W. (2009) The Fretful Euro Disneyland. *International Journal of Marketing Studies.*1 (2)87-91

www.ingramcontent.com/pod-product-compliance
Lightning Source LLC
Chambersburg PA
CBHW051327170526
45166CB00002B/709